EXECUTIVE
Etiquette
POWER

Twenty Top Experts Share What to Know
To Advance Your Career

POWER**D**YNAMICS PUBLISHING

PowerDynamics Publishing
San Francisco, California
www.powerdynamicspub.com

ISBN: 978-0-9644906-4-2

Library of Congress Control Number: 2009907938

Printed in the United States of America on acid-free paper.

We dedicate this book to you, the CEO, salesperson, business owner or young professional just getting started, who recognizes the power of knowing what to do and when to do it to be most effective. We salute you for embracing etiquette to advance your career—and we celebrate your commitment to being the best you can be!

The Co-authors of *Executive Etiquette Power*

TABLE *of* CONTENTS

ACKNOWLEGEMENTS

Gratitude is an important part of executive etiquette. Before we share our wisdom and experience with you, we have a few people to thank for turning our vision for this book into a reality.

This book is the brilliant concept of Caterina Rando, the founder of PowerDynamics Publishing and a respected business strategist, with whom many of us have worked to grow our businesses. Working closely with many etiquette professionals, she realized how much she was learning about communication, behavior, and how etiquette can enhance one's career. The result was putting our ideas into a comprehensive book.

Without Caterina's "take action" spirit, her positive attitude and her commitment to excellence, you would not be reading this book, of which we are all so proud.

Additionally, all of our efforts were supported by a truly dedicated team who worked diligently to put together the best possible book for you. We are truly grateful for everyone's stellar contribution.

To Linda Jay Geldens, whose experience in copywriting, and in copyediting over 50 books proved very valuable, and whose magic pen and expertise ensured that this book would be the best it could be.

To LynAnn King, whose positive energy, creativity and public relations savvy provided valuable support, we are truly grateful.

To Ruth Schwartz, with her many years of experience and wisdom, who served as an ongoing guide throughout the project, your support to our production team and to all of the co-authors is deeply appreciated.

To Barbara McDonald, who brought her creative talent to the cover design and book layout, thank you for your enthusiasm, problem solving and attention to detail throughout this project.

To Bernie Burson, who provided us with a keen eye and an elegant touch, thank you for your support and contribution.

We also acknowledge each other for delivering outstanding information, guidance and advice. Through our work in this book and with our clients, we are truly committed to enhancing the careers of professionals through the use of etiquette and other relevant skills that surround it. We are truly grateful that we get to do work that we love and make a contribution to so many in the process. We do not take our good fortune lightly. We are clear in our mission—to make a genuine contribution to you, the reader. Thank you for granting us this extraordinary opportunity.

The Co-authors of Executive Etiquette Power

INTRODUCTION

Congratulations! You have opened an incredible resource, packed with great ideas that will enhance your career in ways you cannot yet imagine. You are about to discover the exquisite magic of *Executive Etiquette Power.*

Your executive or professional success comes as the result of more than talent, commitment and hard work. Your career success will also be determined by how you greet a client, conduct a meeting, deliver a presentation or entertain your new business contacts. In fact, your success is determined by the way you present yourself in all that you say and do! We know you want to be the absolute best you can be.

With this book, you can quickly learn how leaders in your field conduct themselves to get the very best results. As top experts in each of our respective specialties, we've joined together to give you the most powerful executive etiquette information and strategies available.

Each of us has seen how even small changes in behavior and professional demeanor can transform and uplift your career.

- Knowing how to graciously conduct a meeting boosts your self assurance like nothing else.
- Learning a few networking tips and knowing how to navigate a corporate cocktail party will ensure success the next time you attend a social business function.

- Knowing how to use your silverware correctly, and mastering other dining etiquette details will present you with poise and finesse and give your clients confidence.

- Being the only one at your firm knowledgeable about the etiquette practices of welcoming and conducting business with international clients will give you the advantage you need to stand out when it counts.

All the etiquette professionals you will meet in this book want you to present yourself in the best possible way. We have outlined for you our top tips and included the most expert advice we have to advance your career.

To get the most out of *Executive Etiquette Power,* we recommend that you read through it once, cover to cover. Then go back and follow the advice that applies to you, in the chapters most relevant to your current situation. Every executive etiquette improvement you make will make a difference in your confidence and effectiveness and will impact how others respond to you in your daily professional life.

Know that just learning what to do will not transform your career. You must take action and apply the strategies, tips and tactics we share in these pages. Apply the many skills in this book and you will reap many rewards. With our knowledge and your action, we are confident that, like our thousands of satisfied clients, you too will master the magic of *Executive Etiquette Power.*

To your unlimited success!

The Co-authors of Executive Etiquette Power

The Power of Social Capital

Why Civility and Etiquette are Critical to Your Professional Success

By Deborah King, AICI CIP

People do business with those they know, like and trust. In fact, people will drive farther and spend more for a similar product if they know they will be treated well. Consider those who are willing to spend more for a cup of coffee at Starbucks® when they could get a similar cup elsewhere for much less. Successful businesses work on building their social capital as much as they work on building their products and services.

Social capital concerns how people interact with one another. Businesses and individuals create social capital through the relationships they build. These relationships spawn valuable networks that unite people and can be used to solve problems, generate business, and promote innovation. The common wisdom that people get their jobs from who they know rather than what they know reflects the value of social capital. Building social capital requires strong social skills.

> *"Your bearing, manners and behavior in any business situation largely determine your success or failure."*
>
> —Brian Tracy, best-selling author and professional speaker

Businesses that maintain a culture of respect, goodwill, trust and tolerance are equipped to serve a global community and weather economic storms. Employees who embrace these ideals possess a level of confidence, poise and professionalism that is highly desired and sought after. Your ability to meet and greet others, work a room, dress appropriately, host a business lunch and communicate effectively with others is vital to your business success. Without strong social skills, you will lose opportunities no matter how professionally talented or intellectually smart you are.

There is a shift in today's business landscape. Community-based businesses that served local customers with goods and services needed for daily life are disappearing. There was a time when business owners, employees and customers knew each other by name and shared similar values and life experiences. Hours of operation were confined to Monday through Friday, 9 a.m. to 5 p.m. Weekends were considered sacred and would never be interrupted with business. Weekends were spent with family and friends.

Today's workplace is far more complex and consuming. Technology has expanded business opportunities far beyond our city limits, allowing our products and services to reach a global community. Face-to-face interaction with customers has been replaced with email addresses and automated voices. Multiple generations and cultures sometimes collide in a virtual space that never closes. Years of experience no longer guarantee top pay and privileges. Long-term loyalty no longer ensures a seat at the boardroom table.

Your personal upbringing may have served you well with the skill set you have developed to this point, but you must acquire new skills to advance in your career. Simply possessing technical expertise does not guarantee that you will be promoted to a leadership role. Savvy professionals and corporate leaders understand the business value of social capital. Social capital supports healthy relationships with co-workers and clients. Unfortunately, these skills are not usually taught in our educational system. You must be responsible and proactive in learning the skills to develop your own social capital in order to ensure your career success.

Executive Etiquette Power lays out valuable information that will assist you in increasing your social capital. To begin, I will provide you with a working knowledge of what civility is, how the rules of etiquette apply, and how cultural and generational differences influence your perspective. I will also address the need for being authentic, and how you can apply these skills to real-life career situations.

A Civil Foundation

Civility is the foundation upon which all healthy relationships are built, and thus is necessary for cultivating social capital. Dr. P.M. Forni, author and cofounder, in 1997, of the Johns Hopkins Civility Project, identifies the three R's of civility as respect, restraint and responsibility.

Quality leaders have the capacity to empathize with others. They maintain a high level of respect for themselves, for others and for the work environment. They exercise restraint in their actions and communications, and act responsibly, regardless of who is watching. Incivility is demonstrated by personal attacks on others, gossip, rude or aggressive behavior, dismissive attitudes and general obliviousness toward the impact one's actions have on others. In fact, incivility is the silent killer of relationships.

"Civility-based relational competence is the foundation upon which today's smart and effective executives build their professional success."

—P.M. Forni, Johns Hopkins University

As a business leader, you demonstrate civility when you think the best of others, communicate with consideration and kindness, acknowledge and respect the contributions of others, prize global diversity, dress appropriately for the situation, honor commitments, respect the boundaries and viewpoints of others, provide constructive and kind feedback when solicited and graciously apologize when necessary.

A healthy business community cannot exist without civility.

Etiquette—The Rules for Social Interaction

Etiquette concerns the rules for social interaction; it is the "how-to" for handling various situations. Such rules identify things like whose name you should say first when introducing others, which fork to use and when, the details of politely sending an email or thank-you note, or how to arrange seating for a business meeting.

Every successful social interaction follows appropriate rules of conduct. These rules often are not written, but exist nonetheless. Those who play by the rules succeed and those who don't are silently shunned. Interestingly, rarely does anyone tell you when you have violated one of these rules. Instead you will find that opportunities simply do not come your way.

Since rules can come across as harsh and elitist and make others feel uncomfortable, they must be built on a foundation of civility and empathy. Mastering good manners not only makes you feel more confident, it creates a climate where others feel more comfortable with you.

The Divergence of Business and Social Etiquette

Social etiquette has long been viewed as the guide for polite behavior. The rules for social etiquette are based on age and gender, and preference is given to women and to the elderly. Examples of social etiquette are seen when a young person offers their seat to an older person, or when a man rises from the dinner table to seat a lady.

Etiquette changes as society changes. As more women entered the workplace, new rules for social interaction in the business context were needed. No longer was it acceptable for a man to open the door for a woman at work simply because she was a woman, nor was it appropriate to offer a seat to someone simply because he may be older than you.

Business etiquette defines the new rules of social interaction within the business context. Preference is now based on your position in the business community. For example, a savvy junior staff member would open the door for a senior staff member, regardless of age or gender.

"Good business etiquette speaks volumes, and attention to it will raise the bar for anyone who takes the time."

—Christine Allison, President, D Magazine Partners

Those who only know social etiquette often find it challenging to know what is appropriate in a business setting. Men raised with a knowledge of social etiquette often ask me, "Deborah, do I open the door for a lady or not? I never know if she is going to be offended by my action." The friction caused by social change makes the appropriate choice of behavior more complicated. In every social situation you face, you should pause and consider who you are with, what their frame of reference may be, and then consider how the rules of etiquette may be applied in a way that would best enable you to build bridges—not barriers—with others. This decision must be based on kindness and consideration for all.

The Influence of Culture

Every culture embraces its own rules for social interaction. In my home, slurping your soup is seen as rude, but in Japan, slurping your soup is considered polite because it communicates pleasure and gratitude to your host. Ignorance of cultural differences can create confusion, misunderstandings and loss of business opportunities.

Advancement in your career will require a working knowledge of appropriate behavior and dress in various cultures. Successful businesses embrace a global perspective. If your work includes interaction with clients or colleagues of a different culture, be diligent in learning about their culture and the business rules of conduct that their culture dictates. In this book we have included a chapter on international etiquette by Listi A. Sobba on page 203 because we feel it provides crucial information for your career effectiveness. We could not include a chapter on every single country's culture; however, we have included two of the most relevant for business today. See Syndi Seid's chapter, *Eight Good Luck Tips for Proper Chinese Etiquette,* on page 215 if you have Chinese clients, and read Sangeeta Sindhi Bahl's chapter on *The Art of Doing Business in India* on page 227 if your business takes you to India.

Four Generations in the Workplace

Etiquette is influenced by the generation in which you were raised. Generational heritage provides the perspective from which you view others, and cross-generational conflicts can be traced to different conceptions of appropriate behavior.

Today's workplace is richly diverse, embodying four generations. Each generation not only brings their talent and technical expertise to the office, but also their life perspective that has been shaped by the news, music, heroes and entertainment to which they have been exposed. Previously, generational mixing was uncommon. Senior staff with age and experience typically held upper-level positions, while those who were younger and had little experience held entry-level positions. This created a natural buffer between the generations, as well as a natural progression for advancement.

Generational mixing rose in frequency as technology became more commonplace. The Gen X's and Gen Y's cut their teeth on technology, while many Traditionalists and Boomers initially resisted, or struggled to master sending an email. This newly valued technical knowledge opened doors to the younger staff for upper-level positions in the workplace. Although strong technically, younger workers do not have the years of experience that senior staff possess. Senior staff members often express frustration with younger workers: "Young people today have no work ethic. They are nothing more than 5:01ers. They arrive at 9 a.m. and leave promptly at 5:01 p.m., even if there is a project deadline." Meanwhile, the 20-somethings are texting each other their own version of the story: "What's up with management? They are workaholics! They really need to get a life."

Cross-generational teams that operate effectively benefit the organization. One of your professional goals could be to improve your ability to bridge the generational gap. This achievement will elevate your business profile.

To evaluate your cross-generational skills, ask yourself:

- Do you mix socially and professionally with all four generations?
- Do you practice good listening skills?
- Do you value opinions that differ from your own?
- Are you open to new ideas?
- Do you look for opportunities to work with a variety of people?
- When leading a team, do you include multiple generations?

Stress, resentment and frustration are the result of not understanding and valuing another's perspective. When each individual is recognized and respected, the organization is able to benefit from differing viewpoints and provide the best products and services for the marketplace.

Polished, Not Plastic—The Art of Being Authentic

The value of social capital depends on its authenticity. Nothing is worse than being in the presence of someone who is putting on airs in order to impress others. The only person they impress is themselves; their plastic veneer melts in the presence of authenticity.

When you operate with authentic kindness, you see every person as valuable and are cognizant that every action you take somehow impacts others. Polite behavior never makes others feel inferior or degraded. You may strongly disagree with another person's perspective, but you still honor them as a person.

I am often asked if I practice good manners all the time. While I am far from perfect, I do strive to not just "do" polite acts, but rather to "become" them. Only when these skills become automatic and part of who you are will they truly be useful.

"Etiquette is not about separating the educated from the uneducated or the affluent from the masses, but a product of the human brain at its best, understanding the needs of others and bringing mankind together."

—Horacio Sanchez, President, Resiliency, Inc.

Handling Difficult Situations

Imagine that your boss has just handed you an impossible task and you are angry. You promptly sit down at your computer and start typing an email to a co-worker, passionately describing your frustration. You explain in detail how rude and thoughtless your boss was, and that you plan on looking for another job. As soon as you hit the send button, you realize that you accidentally sent the email to your boss, not your co-worker. You sit stunned for a few minutes and then start thinking about what you should do.

Here is a five-step action plan to handle difficult situations:

1. Consider everyone who may be impacted by the situation.
2. What are the possible actions that you could take?
3. What would be the result of each of those actions?
4. Which action would be the best for everyone involved?
5. Apply that action.

In the above situation, those impacted would be your boss, possibly your co-worker and of course, you.

Possible actions may include: ignoring the situation, asking technical support to retrieve the email, trying to get to your boss's computer to delete the message yourself, sending another email apologizing, calling and apologizing, or going to his office and speaking to him directly.

By ignoring the situation, you are only putting off the inevitable. By trying to find a way to delete the message from his computer, you may create new problems for yourself and others. By sending an email, making a telephone call, or going to him in person, you would be personally addressing the issue.

The best course of action would be to go to your boss immediately and apologize in person. It would also be good to establish a personal policy never to send an email when you are, or the content of your message is, emotional.

Lead by Example

Respected leaders model excellence in all they do. Your ability to read the situation you are in, to understand the people you are with, and to identify the goals you would like to achieve, will enable you to more effectively build positive relationships and will set you apart in the business community.

Excellent business behavior will open doors that money, position, power or an Ivy League education never will. Today's workplace requires you to have strong interpersonal skills that will enable you to bridge the gap between cultures, genders and generations. The skills that brought you to this point in your career will not be sufficient to take you to the next level in business. You must work to continually increase your social capital. The effort you put forth to polish your social skills will reap immense rewards.

DEBORAH KING, AICI CIP
Final Touch Finishing School, Inc.

(206) 510-5357
deborah@finaltouchschool.com
www.finaltouchschool.com

Deborah King is President of Final Touch Finishing School, Inc., which she founded in Seattle, Washington in 1989. Deborah is an AICI Certified Image Professional whose passion is to help others project the best image possible. Her customized programs equip people from all walks of life with the necessary skills to be able to move confidently from informal to formal situations with ease and grace.

Deborah's specialized training includes: The Emily Post Institute, Protocol School of Washington®, Conselle Institute of Image Management, and IAPC Executive Etiquette Education. She is a member of the Association of Image Consultants International, National Association of Professional Women, International Association of Protocol Consultants and the National Speakers Association.

Deborah is a published author as well as a reliable resource to the media. She is a national and international speaker who is highly acclaimed for her expertise and warm teaching style. She presents to diverse organizations and corporations such as the University of Washington, Sam Noble Foundation, Microsoft, Boeing, Hilton Hotels and Cobb, Fendley & Associates. Since 2003, she has consulted for the prestigious Meadowood Resort in Napa Valley, California.

The Psychological Power of Embracing Executive Etiquette

By Suzanne Zazulak Pedro

As a society, we employ etiquette to create guidelines for appropriate conduct. In business, you need to know not only what to expect, but the meaning behind others' actions. To be a successful executive, you will greatly benefit from having a vast knowledge of human behavior and effective communication skills, both verbal and nonverbal. Understanding the psychology of etiquette, and being able to effectively use certain tools such as eye contact, physical positioning and mirroring are key to your success. In addition, observing and interpreting certain things about human behavior can be invaluable in business.

Keeping Your Eyes on the Prize

Historically, the eyes have been described as "the windows to the soul." Chinese jade dealers purposely wore glasses when evaluating stones for purchase. They knew that their eyes could reveal the degree of their interest in a particular stone and might hinder their negotiation skills.

It is true that most people will judge others in the first two to three seconds of an initial meeting. You might think that you make rapid-fire interpretations of people because of your experience in the fast-paced, information-overloaded world that is constantly bombarding you with multi-tech stimuli. But those initial judgments are actually an innate biological function that is critical to our survival, whether in the real jungle or the concrete version.

Since the eye absorbs the first clues before the brain synthesizes our reaction, highly respected professionals in pursuit of success make sure to maintain good eye contact, especially in a first meeting. Charismatic professionals know instinctively what Leil Lowndes said in her book, *How to Talk To Anyone*, published in 2003 by McGraw-Hill, that Yale researchers have validated that more eye contact creates more positive feelings about the person who is looking at you.

The response we have to someone's profound gaze also has a biological base, as it is similar to the mechanism that operates when we fall in love. The body responds with an increased heartbeat, releasing a drug-like substance called phenylethylamine into our nervous system. This substance is the hormone detected in the human body during erotic excitement.

As an executive, your knowledge of oculesics—the study of eye contact—is a powerful tool for success. For example, one technique you can use to decipher an employee's or a client's reaction to certain ideas is dubbed "Epoxy Eyes," according to Leil Lowndes.

This technique is employed when at least three people are present—you, your target, and another person. Traditionally, when someone is speaking, you are focused on that person. With Epoxy Eyes, you steadily direct your gaze toward the listener, your target, rather than toward the speaker.

This puts the listener—your target—on the defensive, wondering why you are so preoccupied with them. Your target becomes keenly aware that you are interested in their reactions. This technique can be very beneficial when it would be advantageous for you to judge the listener.

Epoxy Eyes emits signals of interest, combined with a confident aura. This projects a powerful first impression, which is a sign of respect and conveys that you care about what others think. You are giving the first compliment. However, this may be too intense. In a less intense version, you watch the speaker but redirect your glance to your target each time the speaker finishes a point. This version will allow the target to feel you are intrigued by their reactions, but there is some relief from the intensity of the gaze.

Oculesics can help you advance your skills at reading nonverbal eye clues.

As a rule of thumb, maintain eye contact with your client two-thirds of the time with seven seconds of gaze, then direct your gaze away for three seconds. However, eye contact is not limited to the eye alone. True eye contact concentrates on anything in the "eye-nose" triangle—focus on this area 65-70 percent of the time.

Do be aware of cultural sensitivity regarding direct eye contact. In Japanese culture, for example, lowering the eyes and indirect eye contact are the norm.

Pupil Metrics

Another way you can determine if your client is interested is to look at their pupils. Large advertising agencies, as well as research and development firms, often employ pupil metrics. They can determine how the average consumer reacts to certain product packaging by measuring pupil dilation.

Your pupils will enlarge when you are frightened or when you like something or someone. This is an evolutionary bodily response that allows the body to absorb more information from the environment. Even if the area is well lit, your enlarged pupils will let more light into your field of vision.

When someone looks at you and their pupils get large and black, they either fear you or like you. Although it is almost impossible for a person to control his or her pupil size, you can use this situation to your advantage with effective lighting. Bright, direct lighting will diminish pupil diameter, making you look less attractive, while low lighting will give the pupils the opportunity to dilate, thereby creating "likeability." This is the reason why people always seem more attractive by candlelight.

A Blink of an Eye

Blinking is another feature of the eye that is very telling about behavior. Used primarily as a biological response for keeping the eyeball lubricated, blinking can also indicate deception. A person blinks 7-15 times per minute on average. However, under pressure or when being deceptive, a person's blink rate will increase 5-12 times that number.

For example, take former President Clinton during the Monica Lewinsky situation. Although his normal blink rate pattern was 7-12 blinks per minute, during his apology and denial speech, Clinton's blinks were recorded at 70 per minute. On a higher level, he was unconsciously uncomfortable and deceptive in his communication.

Repeated blinking could also be attributed to allergies, irritants or tics. It is the rare individual who never blinks.

Here are additional ideas for successful eye contact:

- Women engage in more eye contact than men. Women who have a large amount of eye contact tend to be more self-disclosing about personal subjects.

- When eye contact decreases, men tend to disclose more and women tend to disclose less.

- The longer the eye contact, the more a person is perceived to have high self-esteem.

- A woman who wants to make a good impression on a male client should look at a man from head to toe with steadfast eye contact.

- A man who wants to make a good impression on a female client should look at a woman from the shoulders up.

- Blue eyes are more compelling for eye contact. A blue-colored pupil is much easier to notice, and compels others to stare.

- People look away faster from brown eyes. Since it is harder to discern pupil dilation and interest, a brown-eyed individual requires a conscious gaze.

- Tilting your head to the right when speaking inspires trust and confidence. Tilting your head to the left inspires attraction.

Kevin Hogan, author of *Covert Hypnosis*, published in 2006 by Network 3000, as well as other psychological researchers, arrived at a consensus that 55 percent of a first impression is based on nonverbal communication, primarily due to the subliminal leaking of micro-expressions, fleeting expressions that take place in perhaps 1/25th of a second. Most people are unaware of how their words contradict their micro-expressions. For example, consider the reaction of the President of France's wife, Madame Sarkozy, to President Obama upon their first meeting. She flashed him her most charming smile in an effort to appear welcoming and happy to greet him, yet her body language expressed her wanting to keep her distance.

These nonverbal clues are filtered very quickly when you make a decision about someone's "likeability" quotient. The knowledgeable executive will look for nonverbal clues to optimize their communication skills that form the backbone of etiquette.

Use Space to Change Perception

Within the first ten seconds of meeting, a client can determine if you approve of them by your physical distance from them. As discussed in the 5th edition of *Nonverbal Communication in Human Interaction*, by M.L. Knapp & J. A. Hall, published in 2007 by Wadsworth, in 1966, sociologist Edward Hall discovered the dynamics of space as it relates to human interactions. The term "proxemics" is used to describe the study of how humans interact within their space.

The parameter of an individual's space is known as their "intimate space," usually defined by an 18-inch bubble around a person. Unless you strategically want an unhappy outcome, stay outside a stranger's "intimate space." In the 2004 presidential candidate debate between Al Gore and George W. Bush, remember how Gore consistently got up from his chair, crossed the stage and approached the President in his "intimate space"? The result was that President Bush and the viewers interpreted Gore's actions as rude, aggressive and insensitive.

The ideal range for initial contact begins at four feet and diminishes to two feet for familiar contacts. Research shows that the best psychological position for first impressions would be to stand slightly to the right of the other person. This allows the client's right eye to link with the left side of his brain—the lobe of thought. Because the right brain elicits anxious instinctual emotions, positioning yourself to the client's left can cause apprehension and uneasiness.

Another aspect of positioning is the approach, which is a determining factor in making a first impression. The best position for either a man or a woman is to point your feet and your body in the client's direction. Conversely, if the client's feet and body point away from you, the message is that they are not open to you.

Men do not prefer a face-to-face approach, which is interpreted as too confrontational. A man's preference is to stand at a 90-degree angle to their conversational partner.

Women would rather be approached from the front. They seek more direct eye contact in order to gauge if someone might be dangerous or an adversary.

Where You—and Others—Sit Counts

Did you know that seating selection shouts volumes about your power and the value of your opinions? Executives can use proxemics to learn how to change perceptions of themselves with different seating arrangements. Most elected group leaders seat themselves directly at the leadership position at the head of rectangular tables. Also, in mock juries, the person seated at the end position is more likely to be chosen as the leader.

To establish cooperation and equality, the traditional "peace-maker" round table will promote diplomacy and is excellent for brainstorming or other high-energy projects. The circle has no position of authority.

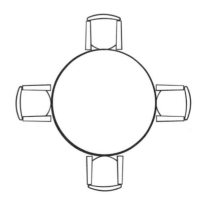

When you need mutual cooperation to come to a consensus, use the "roll-up-your-sleeves" or side-by-side position. Tonya Reiman—in *The*

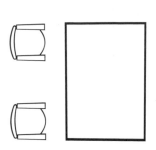

Power of Body Language, published in 2007 by Pocket Books— indicated that people tend to work harder to come to mutually agreeable solutions in this configuration. If you have a partner, you as the executive should position yourself to his or her right. This will unconsciously convey that you can be trusted.

Try angular seating for persuasion, conversation or even seduction. This allows visual contact with no furniture, or without much distance between you and the other person. In fact, if the client places an object between you, such as a briefcase, it is an indication that they wish to separate or distance themselves from you.

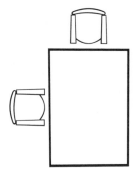

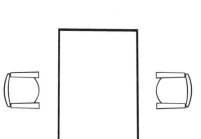

Sometimes the situation warrants a more competitive, more confrontational approach. In this scenario, you would choose a position directly opposite from a competitor. Lawyers often use this adversarial seating arrangement.

If you are in a coach or teacher role, position yourself in the middle of the right side of the table. This is an excellent seat from which to elicit all opinions in a non-threatening manner. Research discussed in Tonya Reiman's book, *The Power of Body Language,* indicates people in this position also speak more, since all eyes are focused on them.

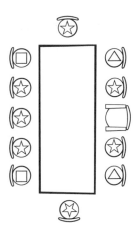

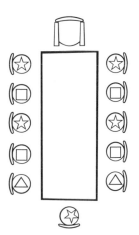

On certain occasions, for example when you come unprepared for a meeting, less visibility may be more valuable. As an executive at a high-ranking meeting, where you sit can have great impact on others' perception of you. In this illustration, each star denotes places that are likely to make you more visible and give you a "seat at the table."

The square positions in this illustration are viewed as neutral. These are people who do not want to be actively involved in a discussion. The triangle positions are the "meeting camouflage" seats, where you can simply fade into the woodwork.

Using Movement and Position Effectively

In the sphere of social space, how can you use movement for strategic advantage? Strategic movement, also known as "spatial anchoring," is a powerful nonverbal process. It can be useful in various business scenarios, such as sales, persuasive speaking and fundraising, and is a great tool for presenting your ideas memorably in front of a group.

Prior to delivering a presentation, take time to evaluate and get comfortable with your venue. Select three specific points on-stage from which you will speak.

Point A will be the podium. Presidents, professors and people in authority deliver their message from the podium. Use this position to deliver factual information to your audience.

Approximately four feet to the left of the podium is Point B, or the "bad news" point, where you speak about problems or anything perceived as bad.

Point C will be approximately two feet to the right of the podium. All information delivered from this position is motivating or uplifting.

So how does etiquette fit into this scenario? People resent strong-arm tactics or being bullied into their decision-making process, and overt behavior is sometimes interpreted as being rude and aggressive. To increase your level of success when speaking to a group, develop a good rapport with your audience; don't alienate them. Using spatial anchoring will eliminate any adverse feelings, and you will be able to easily persuade your audience to accept your point of view.

As an executive, remembering to employ these beneficial tactics and the rules of seating etiquette can be a challenge, but when utilized they will significantly contribute to your success.

Mirroring for Profit

Successful rapport comes from using nonverbal communication skills such as oculesics, proxemics and spatial anchoring.

As the saying goes, imitation is the sincerest form of flattery. Rapport occurs when you match other people's behavior, particularly their pacing. You must be willing, and flexible enough, to enter someone else's reality. This can be achieved through the bond-building technique of isopraxism or mirroring. People like people who are like them. So, be just like your client.

The first step to pacing involves the rate, tone and pitch of your voice. To effectively pace, match your client's breathing rhythm and their posture. Pacing is a process, like etiquette, that creates comfort for your client. Remember, people do not buy ideas, products or services—they buy you!

Isopraxism, or mirroring, can be your secret weapon for easily and immediately establishing rapport. For example, whether you are in a one-on-one interview or at a client meeting, casually notice the other person's body movements. During your discussion with a client or employee, if they touch their face, clasp their hands or whatever, if you mirror them with similar actions, that will trigger a physiological response in their body, reinforcing the warm feelings that come from familiarity.

It is this sense of familiarity that creates the subconscious feeling, "I like this person because they seem just like me." Caveat: Make sure your gestures are neither grandiose nor mimicking.

Time to Communicate More Consciously

The successful individual, regardless of occupation, has mastered the secrets of communication. Ways to enhance every interaction are no longer a mystery, but rather a mastery of your ability to observe and use verbal and nonverbal communication skills. Applying the psychology of etiquette through the tools and information discussed in this chapter will give you executive etiquette power that you can bank on in every professional situation.

SUZANNE ZAZULAK PEDRO
The Protocol Praxis, LLC

(985) 974-0947
suzanne@theprotocolpraxis.com
www.theprotocolpraxis.com

Suzanne Zazulak Pedro's first foray into the world of etiquette was her emergence into her Southern heritage of elegance, pageantry and the adherence to tradition. Born in New Orleans, Louisiana, she has traveled extensively and has had the opportunity to participate in a wide range of different global customs.

Certified by The American School of Protocol in corporate and children's etiquette, she holds a Bachelor of Arts in Psychology from Loyola University, with graduate studies in forensics and law. As CEO of The Protocol Praxis, LLC, and as a behavior-shaping specialist, she has combined the art of social finesse with the tenets of psychology, resulting in "avant garde" etiquette.

Besides being Chief Officer of Protocol for her city, Hammond, Louisiana, she has formed a non-profit organization, Bee Poised, to help children less fortunate learn valuable life skills.

Suzanne's professional memberships include The International Society of Protocol and Etiquette Professionals, Protocol Diplomacy International and the Protocol Officers Association. She writes a monthly etiquette column for several publications, is an expert author on ezinearticle.com, and volunteers as an etiquette and social graces expert for allexperts.com.

Getting a Business Relationship Off to a Good Start

By Michele Pollard Patrick

The first time you meet someone presents an opportunity that will never come again. This is your best chance to make a good impression. Your words, how you say them and your body language all play extremely critical roles. Therefore, it is to your advantage to make your introduction a good one.

Take control of this process. Look alert. Appear self-confident. Assert yourself. Be the first to extend your hand. A confident introduction is one of the most effective business tools you can have because it sets the stage for all that follows.

You never know when you will cross paths with this person again. What you do know is that the impression you leave will determine whether or not this person wants to know more about you. Give the people you meet a reason to want to get to know you.

The Judgments that People Make

Have you ever met someone and immediately thought, "I really like this person" or "I don't trust this guy"? You have already formed an opinion, but you may not know why. Subconsciously, we judge people in the first seven seconds by the way in which they present themselves.

There are six opinions that people form in the first seven seconds:

- Your level of success

- Your level of intelligence

- Your social position

- Your trustworthiness

- Your confidence

- Your accountability

How can someone make all these judgments in just a few seconds? By the way you present yourself in your introduction. Let's take a look at how you can influence others' opinions during that initial timeframe.

Six Ways to Make Others Want to Meet and Get to Know You

1. The approach. Walk with enthusiasm and purpose. Stand up straight. Look as though your intent is to make a connection. This shows confidence.

2. Stand for all introductions. Standing shows respect for others and says you feel good about who you are.

3. Make eye contact. When you look someone in the eyes, it makes the other person feel that you really want to meet them. Hold your eye contact for about five seconds. If you look away during your introduction, people might perceive you as untrustworthy.

4. Smile. A smile says you are approachable, upbeat and positive. People like to be around others who send positive vibes. Be strategic with your smile. Smile when you extend your hand to show you are cordial and welcoming. Those who smile continuously, however, appear disingenuous.

5. Give a proper handshake. The acceptable handshake in the American business world begins with the extension of your right hand. Because some cultures are offended by the use of the left hand, using the right hand ensures that you will not offend anyone. Make your handshake firm and brief.

6. Say your name. Speak slowly and clearly in a confident voice. This is your opportunity to let others know who you are. If you speak too softly or mumble and people do not understand what you say, you will lose the opportunity to be remembered. If you have a difficult name, repeat it; help others pronounce your name and remember it by using an anecdote. During a training program at Duke University, I introduced myself to a young woman who was a graduate student from overseas. I had difficulty pronouncing her name, so I politely asked her to help me say it correctly. She replied, "I'll do better than that. If you will take a moment to stand behind me, you will always remember that I am Behanme." After many years, I can still remember her name.

Six Strategies to Influence People with Your Handshake

A good handshake is not to be overlooked because it can make or break a good first impression. Follow these strategies to ensure that your handshake enhances people's perception of you.

1. Initiate the greeting. Be the first to approach someone. You are setting the stage. You will create the impression that you are confident, poised and in control. All of these attributes make a favorable impression.

2. Extend your right hand. Present your hand palm perpendicular to the floor and slightly tilted, which conveys that you welcome the introduction.

4. Pump from the elbow. Pump the person's hand two or three times and then hold his hand while you continue your introduction. If instead, you pump continuously throughout the introduction, people will remember the pumps and forget your name.

5. Release. Do not linger in the handholding position, because it can be uncomfortable and intimidating.

6. Follow with a message. Say something that makes others feel good, such as, "It's very nice to meet you."

Correct Handshake

Avoid Handshakes that Can Offend

While a good handshake can solidify a great first impression, certain handshakes can leave an unfavorable one. Be sure to avoid these first impression killers:

• **The Hand Hurter.** This handshake is generally used by someone who feels that the harder you squeeze a hand, the more powerful you are perceived to be. Nothing could be further from the truth. This technique indicates that you are insecure and are overcompensating for your discomfort. The recipient of this painful handshake will not want to shake your hand again and you may lose this contact forever.

The Hand Hurter

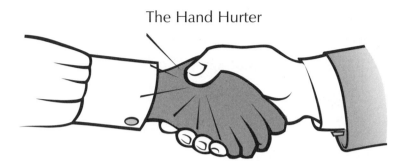

• **The Fingertip Pincher.** This handshake is used by people who are uncomfortable and want to keep you at a distance. It projects weakness and insincerity. It says, "I know I am supposed to meet you, but I really would rather not."

The Fingertip Pincher

• **The Double Hand Hold.** This handshake is rarely used in the United States. It shows superiority and can be perceived as condescending. The only time this may be used appropriately is when you are trying to console someone.

The Double Hand Hold

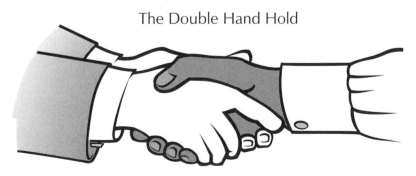

Introductions in business are made with a good handshake, eye contact and a smile. Hugging and kissing are inappropriate because they can be misinterpreted and could lead to negative feelings.

The Art of Introducing Others

Your company is holding a reception for its clients. Robert Smith, your most significant client, has arrived, and you want Tim O'Brien, Chairman of the Board, to know that he is here. You graciously guide Robert in the direction of Mr. O'Brien.

Without skipping a beat, you say: "Mr. O'Brien, I want you to meet Robert Smith, CEO of Clover Construction, which represents a substantial part of our business. Robert, this is Tim O'Brien, our Chairman of the Board."

Question: Is this introduction correct?

Answer: No. While Mr. O'Brien holds the highest title associated with the company, he is not the most significant. Mr. Smith, the client, orders products and services, thereby keeping the company viable. Therefore Mr. Smith is more important in this scenario and Mr. O'Brien should be introduced to him.

Six Basic Rules for Introducing Business Associates

1. Introduce people with comparable positions in no specific order. You may make the introduction either: "John Smith, I'd like to introduce Eric Chen, who is also a sales associate for our company" or, "Eric Chen, I'd like to introduce John Smith, who is also a sales associate for our company."

2. Introduce a "lower ranking" person to a "higher ranking" person. Status is determined by the person's level of position in the company or level of accomplishment. Introductions are made in this order to show respect to the person who has earned the higher position. You will always want to say the more important person's name first: "Tom Rafferty, I'd like to introduce Gary Shorb, an accountant from our Dallas office. Tom Rafferty is our VP of Finance."

3. Introduce a layperson to an official. In this instance, you would say the name of the official person first: "Mayor Jones, I'd like to introduce Abigail Scott, the Senior Vice President of XYZ Corporation, who has been responsible for funding your city project. Abigail, this is Mayor Jones of Chicago."

4. Gender has no preference in business introductions. This rule is contrary to introductions in social settings. In a social setting, a polite gentleman would always be introduced to a lady, like this: "Mary Sullivan, I'd like to introduce Peter Jones." However in business, rank takes precedence. If the gentleman holds a higher position, we would say his name first: "Peter Jones, I'd like to introduce Mary Sullivan, staff writer for the company newsletter. Peter is the Director of Marketing for the Eastern Division."

5. Introduce any guest at a company event to the guest of honor. "Sarah Brown, I'd like to introduce Tim O'Brien, the Chairman of the Board. Sarah is our very deserving honoree this evening."

6. Introduce a fellow executive to a client. "Robert Smith, I'd like you to meet Tim O'Brien, the Chairman of our company. Robert is the CEO of Clover Construction, which represents a substantial part of our business."

Six Savvy Tips about Introductions

1. Business introductions mean more than exchanging names. Part of your responsibility during an introduction is to help those who have been introduced to facilitate conversation. It is helpful to describe each person's position, occupation or reason for being at the event. Doing so enables the parties to begin conversation immediately. They will be grateful for the assistance, and you will be considered a gracious and savvy businessperson.

2. Use first and last names. You may know Barbara well and call her by her first name, but those who are meeting her will want to know her first and last names and something about her.

3. Use titles. It is important for people to know with whom they are speaking. If John Ridgefield is a judge, introduce him as Judge John Ridgefield. If Mary Snow is a doctor, introduce her as Dr. Mary Snow. This courtesy enables people to address others properly and avoid embarrassment.

4. Use honorifics with last names. Sometimes it appears rude to assume that you are on a first-name basis with clients or superiors when you have actually just met them. You will never be criticized for using an honorific such as Mr. or Ms. with a last name. It is the courteous approach. If a client or superior wants you to be on a first-name basis, you will be invited to do so. In the meantime, your words have conveyed honor and respect. It's a win-win situation for everyone.

5. Acknowledge "name blackouts." When you admit that you have momentarily forgotten someone's name, it puts everyone at ease. This happens to all of us. Your acknowledgement has just made it clear that the introduction is more important than your momentary name blackout.

6. Acknowledge family members with different last names. If your spouse has a different last name, remember to acknowledge this in your introduction. I was widowed when my husband and I married. I kept the Pollard name out of respect for my children (who are Pollards), and added Patrick to my name. My name is Pollard Patrick, while my husband is simply Patrick. I always make sure I introduce him as David Patrick so that others will address him correctly. It is not only considerate to my spouse but helps avoid embarrassing moments for those who meet him.

Business Card Etiquette

Brian Garfield has invited a potential client to lunch. His ultimate goal is to encourage an ongoing business relationship. To ensure that the association continues, Brian has his business card ready so he can place it on the table as soon as he and his guest are seated. He wants to be proactive by initiating a way to follow-up.

Question: Was Brian's strategy a good one?

Answer: No. When we invite a client to lunch, the purpose is to socialize and become better acquainted. Brian presented his card too soon. It now looks as though the purpose of this lunch was to market himself and his company. This reflects poorly on Brian. A business card should be used as a method of follow-up and should be presented at the end of the meal, not at the beginning.

Business cards serve a very specific function. When used properly, they enhance your professional image and encourage future contact. When misused, they reflect poorly on you and do not achieve their purpose. Your business card is an extension of you, and reminds people of you long after your introduction. If we look at the business card in this light, we will want to understand how to use it best.

Business Card Strategies that Can Serve You Well

• **Be concise.** Include pertinent information such as your name, position, company, phone, cell, fax and email in an easy-to-read format. Adding superfluous information will only make it more difficult for people to contact you. Use your formal name. If you want to be addressed by your nickname, place it in parenthesis between your first and last names like this: John (Jay) Brown.

• **Choose a specific place to keep your cards.** Keep your cards in your right pocket. When people give you their cards, place them in your left pocket. This will ensure that you do not accidentally hand out a card that belongs to someone else.

• **Keep a clean, fresh supply.** Remember, your business card is a refection of who you are. It's the handshake you leave behind. No one wants to receive a soiled, crumpled card that does not present a professional image. Use a pocket cardholder to keep your cards presentable.

• **Show interest in others' business cards.** When someone hands you their business card, actually look at it and make a comment about the card. People feel honored when you are interested enough to actually read their card. Remember to place it in your left pocket.

• **Be selective.** There is nothing less professional than a businessperson who hands a business card to everyone in the room. Suddenly your card has become a marketing piece and you have damaged your professional reputation.

• **Personalize your card.** Your business card may be used as an enclosure card when you send a gift to someone with whom you do business.

Simply put a line through the front side of your card, and write a personal note on the front or back. Sign it with your first name.

You are now equipped with the social strategies that will make you memorable and successful, beginning with the first time you meet someone. If you follow these suggestions, you will "own" the introduction and success will surely follow. Practice these strategies until they become a habit. When they become a part of who you are, you will project a confident, poised and professional image, and others will want to meet you.

MICHELE POLLARD PATRICK
National Protocol, Ltd.

(301) 654-1291
michele@nationalprotocol.com
www.nationalprotocol.com

Michele Pollard Patrick is a certified Protocol Officer, professional image coach and has been a business etiquette consultant to corporate clients since 1989. She brings in-depth knowledge to her seminar presentations, and is recognized as an expert in the field of business etiquette and government protocol. Michele is the founder of National Protocol, Ltd, a multilevel training organization based in Washington, D.C. Included in her list of private clients are some of Washington's most prominent figures.

Michele is a certified teacher, former corporate trainer for Xerox Corporation and published author. For over 20 years, she has effectively coached corporate and government executives on the interpersonal skills that instill confidence and project professionalism. Her programs have been profiled on network and cable television shows as well as featured in national newspapers and magazines. Fortune 500 companies, government agencies, international organizations, law firms and universities have engaged her services.

Michele is a graduate of Notre Dame College, the Protocol School of Washington® and the Capital Speakers Program. She is a member of the National Speakers Association. She has been elected to Who's Who of Entrepreneurs and the National Association of Professional Women.

Boosting Your Charisma Quotient

Seven Habits of Highly Effective Conversationalists

By Terry Pithers

I love to watch the Academy Awards, especially the pre-ceremony interviews on the red carpet. It gives me a chance to observe the Hollywood stars interacting without the benefit of scripts and editing. Although many stars lose their glow during these unscripted conversations, a few really shine positively.

George Clooney is one such star. It isn't his good looks that make George stand out from the glittering Hollywood crowd. What stands out is his ability to make the other person, whomever he is talking to, feel like they are the most important person on the red carpet. What stands out is his charisma.

In my business etiquette seminars, I often ask people to describe what one single attribute makes someone charismatic. It's no surprise that the most often mentioned trait is the ability to make others feel like the most important person in the room during a conversation.

The dictionary describes charisma as "a special magnetic charm or appeal that inspires enthusiasm, influence, affection or loyalty in others." This ability is available to all of us if we are willing to work at it, regardless of our birth, rank, physical attributes or gifts.

What can you gain from examining and adopting charisma-enhancing habits? All of us engage in conversations throughout our lives, but the ability to have conversations that make you stand out and really connect will heighten the impact that you make as a businessperson.

As a business professional, developing magnetic charm or appeal that inspires enthusiasm, loyalty or affection from people, especially those within your organization, turns you into a dynamic leader. You will become a leader who is more easily able to form coalitions, network across the organization, bridge silos, build consensus, have stronger teams and inspire people.

So what is it that charismatic people do differently? There are seven simple things that set them apart from the crowd. If you adopt these seven habits, you will greatly boost your own charisma quotient and gain more success in your career and in your life.

1. Charismatic Attitude—Adding a Positive Charge

Charismatic people are enthusiastic and passionate about life, their organizations and what they do. They transmit this positive attitude in their interactions and conversations with others.

They talk in positive terms, and even when things are not going well, rather than complain, they put a positive spin on the situation. Their language and tone is enthusiastic, and they are curious to find what other people are interested in or excited about, and to share in that excitement.

When they find pride in their work or passion in others, they mirror and reinforce it with their conversation. Rather than say something mundane like, "That's interesting," they add zest to the conversation with, "You must find that incredibly rewarding!" or "What got you involved in such a fascinating project?"

They use this positive approach across the board with everyone they meet, regardless of social or business position, and greet everyone with equal respect, interest and enthusiasm. This is especially noticeable in how they interact with the junior-ranked employees in their organizations.

Build this into your own approach by repeating as a daily mantra, "I look for the good in everyone I meet." An effective way to practice this empathetic habit is to start applying it universally in your interactions, beginning with store clerks or service people outside your organization.

Recently in a grocery store checkout line, I watched a young cashier bite her tongue and remain calm as she tried to soothe a rude customer. When it came time to ring up my groceries, I commented, "You must be glad all your customers are not like that. I teach customer relationship skills, and you were very good at defusing that situation." Her eyes lit up and she beamed at me. A little acknowledgment made her day and helped reinforce for me the habit of enthusiastically acknowledging everyone we meet.

This habit relates to the leadership skill of "catching people doing something right." When this becomes your standard operating procedure, you will experience stronger teamwork within your organization and people will gravitate to you.

2. Charismatic Listening—I Only Have Ears for You

A downside to technology trends like smart phones, texting, and cell phones is that people have become less skilled in face-to-face conversation. We are so used to multitasking, we are rarely in the moment when we talk to other people. Charismatic individuals buck this trend by practicing active listening. They understand that focusing their complete attention on the other person is one of the strongest rapport-building elements of conversation.

I call this habit "focused listening." People are starved for the experience of feeling really heard. Being really listened to is memorable because it fills their unfulfilled need. People will go away from your conversation feeling better about themselves and feeling better about you.

You can build your focused listening skills by being in the moment and consciously using your body language to demonstrate your focus. For example, rather than remaining seated when someone approaches to say hello or enters a meeting, stand up to shake hands when you speak to the person and lean forward to show interest.

Charismatic people have an open facial expression with a smile that communicates warmth, delight and a healthy self-esteem. If you frown or have a poker face when taking in information, that can make you appear negative and less approachable.

A simple technique for self-assessing your facial expression is to keep a mirror by your phone. I recommend placing a small mirror in an unobtrusive spot so others don't get the impression you are vain or narcissistic. During telephone conversations, this will give you a good sense of how you come across face-to-face so you can work on opening up your expression. As a bonus, the warmth of your smile will increase the charisma of your tone of voice to exude enthusiasm and interest, not only in person but over the phone.

In North America, one of the greatest charismatic body language cues for validating others is looking them in the eye. Most people stop eye contact a bit too quickly after meeting others. If you sense that the other person is uncomfortable with prolonged eye contact, then take a break naturally from time to time by looking away, as though you're deep in thought.

When you're talking to a small group, make sure you engage everyone with eye contact. If this is difficult for you, then work at sharing one thought per person. Good eye contact is important while you are talking, but as a listener it is even more essential to show that you are engaged in the conversation.

Remember the truism: people don't care about you until you show how much you care about them. When you meet someone for the first time you want to listen 80 percent of the time and talk 20 percent. Beyond body language, focused listening is also promoted through verbal cues. In addition to nodding you can add, "Uh-huh," "Go on," or "Yes." You can also ask questions or paraphrase parts of the conversation to indicate you are actively listening.

As a professional speaker, I often have lunch with my conference audience members before my presentations. When I was starting out in my speaking career, I wasted these conversation opportunities because I was too busy thinking about my presentation to fully engage and build rapport.

Now, I embrace these opportunities to use focused listening with my audience members and gain insights and points that will make my presentation stronger. If you get into the habit of implementing this practice when networking with people within your organization, you will be surprised at how others will open up and share their knowledge and experiences. As a leader, this will increase your own profile and knowledge base.

3. Charismatic Introductions—Shining the Spotlight

Charismatic individuals introduce others more effectively than most people do. Because of their natural enthusiasm and interest in others, they will often add a statement or fact to their introduction that helps others connect, or provides a springboard for conversation.

They consistently look for commonalities or similar interests that might connect people. Instead of introducing by rote such as, "This is Mary Jones from Accounting," they will take the trouble to add, "Mary is originally from St. Paul. That's your hometown, isn't it, David?"

You can take this habit a step further. A charismatic leadership skill is to integrate acknowledgment and praise into the introduction of colleagues or employees. I call this "shining the spotlight on others." Introduce someone with phrases like, "This is John Marshall, who will be heading up your project. John's specialty is bringing in complicated projects on time and under budget."

One of my clients, who owns a very successful engineering firm, finds it difficult to brag or blow his own horn. He told me that because he was brought up not to brag, he likes introducing his engineers to clients using the spotlight technique. He comments, "It allows me to brag about my company to the client, while demonstrating recognition of the talents and accomplishments of my engineers."

Unlike flattery, which people usually recognize because it is overt and can feel manipulative, acknowledgment is indirect and more effective. Incorporating this habit into your introductions also builds your reputation that you offer praise in public and criticize only in private.

Members of your team are more likely to share their ideas and provide stronger teamwork to leaders who demonstrate that they share credit and recognition.

4. Charismatic Small Talk—Route 66 to Big Talk

Charismatic conversationalists appreciate the importance of "small talk" as a lubricant that gets the conversation rolling. They understand that "big talk" is not necessarily about business, or serious subjects. They know that when they move the conversation to whatever the other person is interested in or passionate about, they have entered the realm of big talk for that person.

Small talk is a way to explore and discover what the other person considers big talk. One of the most common opening gambits for small talk is the weather. My seminar participants often want to know, "What do I talk about after the weather?" I say listen to how people talk about the weather, or better yet, shift how you talk about the weather.

If someone says, "It sure was a rainy weekend, but at least it was good for my garden," rather than simply replying, "Yeah, it sure was rainy," ask them "What type of garden do you have?" so you can investigate their interest.

Get in the habit of sharing how the weather affects you, thus opening the door to finding out more about the other person. "It was a beautiful weekend. I got in two rounds of golf." The other person should pick up on the cue, but if they don't, you can simply follow up with, "And what about you? What did you do on the weekend—do you golf?"

Many of my clients who are lawyers and accountants with a logical, left-brain outlook have difficulty with small talk. If you fall into this category, it may help to play a mental game of conversational detective. Ask yourself, "I wonder what I am going to learn from this person?" Your goal is to solve the mystery of finding out what the other person is interested in.

When networking within their organizations, charismatic leaders keep their eyes open for visual clues about what their team members value. Think about what is on your own desk or walls: awards, certificates, photos, souvenirs and artwork. When you visit someone's office, their decorations are excellent clues to move small talk into big talk by using simple questions such as, "Where did you get this?" or "How long have your girls played soccer?"

Building relationships in business is never a waste of time. If you don't take the time to enhance the small talk habit in your business conversations, you will never be perceived as charismatic by clients and colleagues.

5. Charismatic Exits—Ending on a High Note

People who are charismatic have a way of incorporating their upbeat positive approach into the way they end conversations in a smooth way that leaves their conversation partners feeling validated. Subconsciously, they associate that good feeling with the charismatic person.

Instead of ending conversations with bland phrases such as, "It was nice talking to you," or "I hope I run into you again," charismatic people will summarize the conversation through a technique I call the "positive recap." They will end on a high note: "That project sounds like a golden opportunity. I'm looking forward to hearing how it turns out when we meet again," or "I enjoyed chatting with you. I didn't realize there was such an art to fly-fishing. I hope to run into you again."

This recap supports and verifies that they were actively listening and can be used at certain points as an invitation to expand the conversation, with statements like, "So you feel that..." or "It sounds like you had a great time in France. Where would you like to have spent more time on the trip?"

For leaders, ending conversations with subordinates with a positive recap, combined with direct eye contact and a smile, is the equivalent of reaffirming, "I value you as a member of my team." It elevates the subordinate's feelings of importance within the organization, and subconsciously elevates your importance as well.

Charismatic leaders will also effectively use this recap technique at meetings. They will start the meeting in a positive manner and will provide an upbeat summary at the end.

6. Charismatic Follow-up—It's All in the Details

We sometimes hear about a politician being praised for his ability to remember constituents' names. Charismatic people tend to focus on remembering details about people, such as their interests. That way, when they reconnect, mentioning a personal detail such as children, hobbies or vacation plans proves they cared enough to remember.

Instead of generically saying, "Good to see you again. How's it going?" the charismatic conversationalist will use a specific reconnection such as, "It's great to see you again. How did your family reunion turn out?"

This habit takes a little bit of work, but the rewards are considerable. When you meet someone again, it takes time to warm up the relationship and re-establish rapport. You can shorten this warm-up period if you can allude to personal details or to the topic of your last conversation. This validates the individual and subconsciously elevates you in their esteem.

An effective technique to help you remember names—and more importantly, the interests of people you meet—is to mentally repeat their name and visualize them engaged in their hobby or interest.

Leaders who inquire of their team members and employees, "How is the job going?" may be seen as caring. Those who are able to couple that with interest in a personalized detail such as, "How did the Little League ball tournament go?" or "How are the Italian lessons coming along?" are seen as being charismatic.

A good contact management system is a prime asset to your charisma. This allows you to keep track of ways in which you can follow up with personal notes and emails that share resources or items of interest. Connect people with other contacts in your world with whom they share commonalities. When you have records of personal interests and the topic of your last conversation, it's easier to nurture relationships.

7. Committing to Charisma—Habitual Habits

Finally, charismatic people make a habit out of practicing their charisma habits. We are not born with these skills. We all have to learn and develop them.

Does developing your charisma factor take effort? You bet, and that is another reason why it will make you will stand out from the crowd. If it was easy, everyone would be charismatic.

When you come across someone you feel is charismatic, analyze what habits they are exhibiting that draw you to them. You are probably using some of these skills and habits now, but like most people, you just don't do them consistently or you do them selectively.

Start working on the habits one by one, and practice on everyone you meet. You'll be amazed at the results. You will more easily influence and arouse enthusiasm and affection in everyone you connect with. You will be seen as a dynamic leader who is capable of inspiring results and allegiance.

TERRY PITHERS
Style for Success

Savvy not stuffy

(780) 472-0767
terrypithers@styleforsuccess.com
www.styleforsuccess.com

Terry Pithers, "The Business Etiquette Guy," is a dynamic speaker, etiquette expert and trainer in soft skills, business dining, business etiquette, networking and conversation. He is a partner in Style for Success Inc., providing valuable tools to business professionals and organizations so they can build stronger and more profitable client relationships.

A member of the Canadian Association of Professional Speakers and the International Federation of Professional Speakers, Terry injects fun and laughter into his presentations. His seminars boast an exceptionally high satisfaction rating among attendees. Terry helps people become "savvy not stuffy."

Understanding that these skills provide a real boost to careers and lives, Terry mentors university law and business faculty students. He has helped a wide range of audiences gain greater success and confidence in their business and personal interactions.

Terry is the co-creator of the *Dining For Success* online video training, which is being used to develop executive table manners by MBA business schools and corporations across North America. He is also the editor of the *Style and Substance* newsletter, available at their website.

Working a Room for Maximum Impact

By Barbara Finney

For many professionals it is exciting to receive an invitation, but as the date approaches, the excitement of attending the event often turns into nervousness and anxiety about meeting new people. Some may hear this little voice inside saying, "Why go? You won't know a single person there, everyone will be busy talking to other people, and no one will notice you." Still, it is important that you go. This is your career, and you want to be out there, connecting with others, and representing your company in the best possible manner. This is a great opportunity to practice your social savvy, meet new people, and build on existing relationships.

Focusing on the power of executive etiquette at networking events can help calm your nerves and relieve anxiety. By following these simple guidelines and concentrating on making others feel comfortable, you will have less time to focus on your own nervousness.

Learn about the People You Will Meet

Spend some time finding out who will be attending the event. Many conferences provide an attendee list, or you can check out association websites. Associations often list photos and biographies of their members.

Google important events going on at the attendees' companies. For example, look for company restructuring, impending mergers, new products, or "green" campaigns. When you meet people at the event, you will feel more confident having something relevant to talk about, and they will be impressed that you have taken the time to learn about them and their company. All of your research will assist you in knowing why you are attending the event, who you want to meet, and what you want to accomplish.

Self-Introduction

Perhaps the most important aspect of your preparation in working a room is your self-introduction. It is a tool that will instantly attract people to you like a magnet, and will very clearly show them the benefits of doing business with you. A great self-introduction is the essential ingredient in building an unforgettable impression of yourself in all your networking efforts. It is as important as having business cards, and in some ways is even more effective. Think about how many hundreds of business cards people collect. They can be forgettable simply because of the sheer numbers we all accumulate. A good self-introduction is anything but forgettable. If you really work on designing a good one, you will be on your new acquaintance's mind for a long time. It is such a great tool for marketing yourself because it works, and best of all, it's free.

A good self-introduction starts with a short, simple, powerful message designed to make people want to know more about you. Explaining what you do needs to have energy—in your voice and body language. You want to make them think, "Why would I want to do business with anyone else?"

A well-prepared, well-rehearsed self-introduction flat-out eliminates the competition. It sells you, and the value of doing business with you. Learn to see yourself as others see you, and understand what they want from a service such as you are offering. A memorable and effective self-introduction will easily move you into further conversation.

People will know exactly what you do, so that there is no confusion. You communicate how you are different from all of your competition, and this lets them see a distinct advantage in doing business with you. Everyone will feel comfortable and relaxed with you and around you. A good self-introduction allows you to use your personality to make a positive impression.

Clearly articulating your self-introduction is very easy to do. Simply ask yourself these five questions: Who are you? What do you do? Whom do you do it for? How do you do it? What happens as a result?

Next, write down all the words, characteristics, ideas and phrases that pertain to each of these questions. Have fun! You will find that your mind is flowing with dozens of key points about yourself. Now it's time to put together those pithy one-liners that will grab attention and intrigue the listener.

For example, a real estate agent might say, "I help couples find the home of their dreams," or a financial planner might say, "I ensure my clients can sleep at night by providing them sound financial advice."

Last but not least, practice, practice, practice. You want this to flow naturally, provide enough impact to arouse interest, and get others to join your word-of-mouth team. With a polished and well-rehearsed self-introduction you can easily take it into the office suites.

Dress Appropriately and Be Distinctive

Plan to make your first impression your very best impression. Within the first few seconds of your appearance, you are evaluated from head to toe, even if just by a glance. Once the first impression is made, it is essentially irreversible. Everything about you should communicate quality and a professional presence.

While different events will call for different attire—and in general, dark colors are recommended, consider being distinctive, making yourself memorable when meeting new people. A brightly colored, hand-painted tie or scarf, unusual jewelry, a good but not overpowering cologne and even flawless grooming will help people separate you from the crowd and remember you. You don't have to be outlandish, but do present yourself so that you don't blend in completely with the crowd.

Always make sure you have plenty of business cards in your pocket. A great tip for both men and women is to wear a jacket with spacious pockets. Why? One pocket will hold your business cards, and another pocket will hold business cards that you collect from others. This eliminates those potentially awkward moments when you are frantically looking for your cards.

Eat Before You Go

Be sure to eat something beforehand so that you don't arrive starving, thirsty and in a rush to grab an hors d'oeuvre or a drink. Remember, networking events are never about the food or beverages.

Focus Your Confidence and Think Positively

Before entering the event room, make a quick trip to the restroom to check your appearance. You will be more relaxed and confident when you are happy with your appearance and know that you look your best.

Check your hair. Does it look good? Are your hands thoroughly washed and dried? Have you popped a breath mint? Is your nametag on the right-hand side? Knowing your appearance is at its best can be priceless!

Take a moment to breathe deeply and focus your confidence. Make sure that your face has a pleasant and approachable expression; keep your chin up and your posture perfect. Do you look and feel like someone you would like to get to know better? Think positively about this opportunity to meet people you don't usually have a chance to meet, and remember you have many things to offer. Now you are ready to make your entrance with an air of confidence and friendliness.

Make a Grand Entrance

A strong entrance announces your presence and helps to establish a positive first impression. As you enter the room, stand tall and walk with a good stride. This will project self-confidence and purpose. Others will see you as being in control of the situation and yourself. Make a purposeful pause—not a long pause, or a pause of hesitation or indecisiveness—but an impressive pause. This will ensure that you don't go unnoticed, and allows you to determine who is present and to whom you wish to speak.

Build Rapport with Body Language

As you are networking, in the first few moments of meeting someone you don't know, you are heavily dependent upon eye contact and open body language to build rapport.

A sincere smile is the surest way to open the door to potential conversations, and you are more likely to build meaningful relationships.

It is important to keep your body straight and tall, with your arms at your sides. Keep your feet in alignment with your upper body so they point to the other person, making them feel important and valued. Never cross your arms, legs or ankles. That will make you appear closed and uninterested in them.

Nodding at the appropriate time is another way to acknowledge the importance of the other person's message.

When you are speaking, use hand gestures and enthusiasm to underscore your key points. They help to emphasize your message and increase the interest level of the other person.

Respect the other person's personal space, which extends approximately an arm's length between conversants, at least in the Western world. Be sensitive to the other's spatial comfort. Violating another's personal space may undermine all previous efforts in building rapport.

Practicing these body language and eye contact skills will help you build and maintain a successful network of relationships to help you achieve your ultimate goals.

Act As If You Belong

Now it's time to show off your social savvy and have fun doing it. It may be a comfort to know that even people who understand the value of networking events often have a difficult time getting over the first hurdle, walking into a room and feeling as if they belong there. As you work the room, you want to act as if you belong. If you start to feel uneasy, use positive self-talk to strengthen your sense of belonging. For example, think of everyone as guests in your home, and act as if you are the host rather than a guest. As the host, you want to approach people instead of waiting to be approached. It is amazing how warm and friendly events seem to be when you engage in this method. Just think about how great you feel when someone takes the initiative to walk up to you and introduce themselves. Extending yourself to others can make you feel like a million dollars when you try it and succeed.

Know Whom to Approach and How Long to Stay

Approaching people can be easier if you scan the room for those you already know so you can easily begin to mingle. If you don't know anyone, find a place where people seem to be congregating and make your way there. Approach groups of three, or find someone who is alone. They will most likely welcome your company, and usually a fourth person will nicely round out a group of three. If you recognize someone from a previous contact, use that to open a conversation. They will appreciate the fact that you remember them. To begin a conversation with someone you don't know, you could say, "Excuse me, may I introduce myself?", or "Excuse me, I could not help but overhear..." Greet people as if you are really glad to meet them. This approach can open up a lot of opportunities.

Arriving early will allow you to meet key people in a less frenzied atmosphere. As the event progresses, they will become very busy, so be respectful of their time, introduce yourself, shake hands, make a good impression and move on.

There are always a lot of people to meet at networking events, so it is a good idea to keep your conversations short—about three to seven minutes. When possible, it is always nice to introduce the person you've been talking with to someone else as you are leaving.

Recognize Personality Styles

It is true that sometimes when you meet someone, you almost immediately feel a connection with him or her—often without any effort. The connection is natural, as if you are kindred spirits. Rapport has been created without even thinking about it. However, other times you meet someone and feel no connection whatsoever. Even when you want to build rapport, for some reason you are unable to. Why are you able to have almost instant connection with some people and almost no connection with others? There are a number of reasons, but the greatest contributor to making a positive connection with others lies in your personality style and the personality styles of others.

As you meet people, you can learn to recognize their personality style by observing their body language. You communicate with your entire being, not just your words. In fact, according to Dr. Albert Mehrabian, a noted researcher in the field of nonverbal communication, the words you speak only account for seven percent of the message. The remaining 93 percent is based on your visual presentation and body language. Making a positive connection with the people you meet rests in your ability to know your own primary personality style, your ability to read the personality styles of others, and knowing how to best relate to each style. There are four primary personality styles to be aware of, and while there are several labeling systems, many books, articles, and profile assessments, I find the DISC behavioral system—the four-quadrant behavioral model based on the work of William Moulton Marston Ph.D. (1893 - 1947)—to be thorough and easy to understand. The four main behaviors of DISC are: Dominance, Influencing, Steadiness and Compliance.

Individuals with a high Dominance profile are the leaders, all about business, task-oriented. Their stance is forward-leaning, and they use lots of hand movements and grandiose gestures. They are quick-paced—always in a hurry. They love change, and will always have the latest gadgets. The Dominant person is not interested in chitchat, but prefers to stick to business, with the facts presented in a logical fashion. In other words—get to the point. Show that you are well-prepared and organized. Ask "what" type questions and provide win-win opportunities.

The Influencing type person has a friendly style, is expressive, charming, people-oriented, and a good mixer. They are very visual, always looking around and using big gestures and fast movements. Their walk is fast-paced, and they are usually multitasking. They speak with passion, and use their hands a lot. The Influencing type person loves socializing, fun and a fast-paced atmosphere. When interacting with them, focus on people and action items. Ask for their opinion, ask "who" type questions and offer personal incentives.

A person with a Steadiness profile is very patient, a good listener, friendly and relaxed. They use moderate gestures, lean back and saunter. They walk with a stroll—never in a hurry. Their dress is never trendy, and they prefer quiet recognition. Begin conversations with a Steadiness type person using chitchat before diving into business. Compliment them, but not in a flamboyant way. Be logical and soft when you present your information to them. Ask them "how" questions and don't be abrupt.

The Compliance profile describes a person who loves facts and details; they are precise, systematic and methodical. They are courteous, diplomatic and have very high standards. Their gestures are very reserved, minimal and contained. They walk in a straight line, and stand with arms folded, or perhaps with one hand on their chin in thought. Approach them in a straightforward way, and don't be too casual. Provide facts and details. Allow them their personal space, and don't touch them—it would be too intimate.

Once you are aware of the four personality styles and traits, your confidence will increase as you learn to read them in others. Reading personality styles is an art that requires practice, but the rewards will increase your personal and professional sphere of influence immeasurably.

Say Goodbye with Grace

Plan your endings just as you planned your self-introduction. Your exit is just as important as your entrance. This will help you politely end one conversation and move on to the next. As you prepare to leave the event, be sure to thank the host and speaker. Say goodbye to everyone you met and briefly reaffirm any commitments you have made.

The essentials for working a room are all about making a positive and lasting impression. Few things happen by accident, so consider going to your next networking performance fully prepared and with style. Relax, have fun and focus on everything you do right.

BARBARA FINNEY
Etiquette Consultant

*Good manners go hand-in-hand
with leadership*

(630) 752-0040
barbara@etiquette-leadership.net
www.etiquette-leadership.net

Barbara Finney is an etiquette consultant based in the Chicago area. Following a successful career as a business analyst and corporate trainer, Barbara followed her true passion of providing etiquette and leadership programs that instill adults and children with knowledge, skill and confidence in manners and etiquette. These are skills that contribute to success for a lifetime. Her positive learning environment is focused on the benefits of giving and receiving respect, and the reassurance of knowing "what to do."

Through workshops, seminars, and personal consultations, Barbara works with clients to perfect their personal and professional presence. Programs are designed around social etiquette, dining etiquette, business etiquette and international protocol. Topics are presented in an interactive and entertaining format, with a blend of professionalism and fun.

As founder and director of the Etiquette and Leadership Institute of Illinois, she has received certification in etiquette and protocol from The Protocol School of Washington®. Barbara is an active member of the Network of Women Entrepreneurs in Chicago.

Your Best Executive Image

Setting the Foundation

By Vonetta Dumas

Your professional image is a combination of your appearance, your behavior and your communication. While executive etiquette is always thought to include communication and behavior, your appearance cannot be overlooked as a key component in conveying trust, professionalism and other traits you want to project in every professional interaction.

The way that you see yourself, however, may differ from the way others see you. As a career-minded person, it is vital that you understand that your physical presentation reflects who you are. In the eyes of those you meet, perception is reality and you must look your best in every business situation, whether it is a first meeting, a luncheon appointment or a company cocktail party.

Your physical image is the basis of how others see you; it sets you apart. You can stand out by doing the little things that make a big difference. Consider the small details that refine your image, which can eliminate what some may consider distractions, like not having manicured nails, cloths that fit, a bright smile or not so perfect teeth. When your image is not in order, people will find it hard to see beyond your well-tailored suit, your hair that is always well-groomed and your beautiful skin to appreciate the talented person behind them. Your image and personal grooming are a key part of your executive etiquette.

Image and personal grooming are vital to your career effectiveness. Here are several important strategies to ensure you a better presentation every time you walk into the office, meet a client or attend a professional event. For more information on your professional image, read *Executive Image Power,* published in 2009 by PowerDynamics Publishing, and available online at www.executiveimagebook.com.

Give Attention to Your Total Grooming

Being well-groomed says that you are conscientious, responsible and detail-oriented. Overlooking your personal grooming sends the message that you are overwhelmed and do not pay attention to detail, and makes you appear unready to take on responsibility.

When you look good, you automatically feel good about yourself and exude a confidence and self-esteem that is recognized and respected, resulting in a positive self-image that will give you the professional and social leverage that you must have in today's competitive society.

You will want to put together a consistent morning self-care regimen that will allow you to efficiently get pulled together and out the door fast. Have your daily essentials like dental care, hair care and skin care products within easy reach. Weekly essentials can be stored away in the linen closet or organized underneath the sink. It is important that you make a weekly inventory to ensure that you have a supply of your key items on hand. There is nothing worse than getting ready for a big day and realizing you are out of toothpaste or antiperspirant.

Time management and organization are vital. Plan today for tomorrow and plan this week for the coming week. Decide what outfits you are going to wear for the coming week based on what events you have on your calendar. Go through your closet and make sure your clothes are clean and pressed, that there are no threads hanging or buttons missing. Doing this ahead of time will allow you to get your mornings started smoothly.

Note: A closet audit, purge and re-organization should be done seasonally to prepare you for the next season.

As you plan for the coming week, also make sure the laundry is done, so that you have enough socks, pantyhose and foundation garments. The whole idea is to set yourself up for a successful week before the week starts, so you do not run out of whatever you need in the middle of your busy schedule.

With all the planning and setting your week up for success, don't forget to take time for yourself. It is essential to create work life balance, and putting yourself first will keep you on top of your executive game. Each morning, get off to a good start by spending a quiet moment with yourself, exercise, eat a healthy breakfast and get yourself out the door on time.

"Women in particular need to keep an eye on their physical and mental health, because if we're scurrying to and from appointments and errands, we don't have a lot of time to take care of ourselves. We need to do a better job of putting ourselves higher on our own 'to do' list."

—Michelle Obama, First Lady of the United States

Be Prepared for Anything

Have you ever noticed a run in your pantyhose just as you step out of your car to enter your office? Noticed a stain on your tie, or popped a button just as you stood up from your desk? Ever spill a beverage on yourself just as you are about to give a presentation? These glitches can ruin your whole day, unless you have an office image survival kit.

Also, if you drive a lot for business, be sure to have an image survival kit in your car. Follow these guidelines to get you out of any compromising image situation.

The Image Survival Kit for Women *Include in a portable tote:*	The Image Survival Kit for Men *Include in a portable tote:*
lint brush	lint brush
sewing kit	sewing kit
safety pins	safety pins
toothbrush	toothbrush
toothpaste	toothpaste
dental floss	dental floss
toothpicks	toothpicks
breath mints	breath mints
deodorant	deodorant
manicure kit with file and nail clippers	manicure kit with file and nail clippers
hand lotion	hand lotion
clear polish	stain remover pen
two pairs of pantyhose	backup necktie
backup pair of shoes	backup shirt
backup shirt or blouse	backup undershirt
stain remover pen	backup blazer
makeup kit	shoeshine kit
hairspray	
panty liners	
sanitary napkins	

Finding Your Best Garment Fit

While it may not be true that clothes make the man—or woman—it is true that a good fit makes any garment look better. A good fit skims the outline of your body's silhouette. When a garment is too snug in a particular place, it pulls or puckers. When a garment is too loose, it hangs, bags and hides your silhouette.

Here is a huge image secret—clothes rarely fit your body best just off the rack. Few people are a perfect fit for their size. You might fit into a size 4, 8 or 12, but that may not be your best fit. Depending on your personal body shape, your jackets may need to be taken in at the shoulders or the waist. Your jacket sleeves may need to be taken up or tapered. You may need to let out your pants at the inseam or take them in at the waist for your best fit.

Determining your best fit is an important project. Hire an experienced image consultant or image management specialist to advise you. When your clothes fit, you always look like they were made just for you. When you buy clothes off the rack without consideration for your unique body shape, you will constantly be tugging at your sleeves, pulling at your buttons or yanking at your hem. All of this is very distracting and takes away from your professional effectiveness.

Answer these questions when purchasing a garment to help ensure a good fit:

- Do the shoulder seam and the grain of the sleeve line up perfectly?
- Do the vertical seams in a garment fall straight, with no pulling?
- When you try on a garment, are there horizontal lines puckering along the back? If so, that means the garment is too small.

When you try on a jacket, check the width of the sleeves. Especially in a plus size, the sleeves are often too large and can make you look bigger.

You should be able to stretch your arms forward comfortably in a jacket that fits well.

Button the jacket and swing your arms up over your head and back down. The jacket should fall back to where it was without needing adjusting. If it does not, it should be taken out a bit. Sometimes even a half-inch alteration makes a huge difference in the fit of a garment. Finding the perfect fit is determined by your proportions, height and figure. Embrace who you are and be empowered by making informed decisions about accentuating and minimizing your figure, where appropriate.

> *"This is not an issue of size, as in your size. This is an issue of the size and shape of your garments and whether they work to accentuate all the things you are."*

—*A Guide to Quality, Taste & Style* by Tim Gunn with Kate Moloney, Abrams Image, 2007.

For women, height is also a major influence on what style of clothes would be ideal.

• Petite: 5'2" and under

• Average: 5'3"—5'7"

• Tall: 5'8" and up

If you are petite or tall, do not shop where average clothes are sold unless you do in fact have access to a master tailor. You give yourself a great head start on looking your best when you buy clothes that are the closest off-the-rack fit for your body.

Many well-dressed men know something that women who want to always be well-dressed would be well-served to learn. The best suit is one that was made just for you. The custom-made suit will always fit you best and you will be sure that no one else around the boardroom table will have the same suit as you. While custom suits are more expensive than ready-to-wear suits, they will always ensure a great fit, and as the name suggests, a custom look. Consider investing in one or two custom-made suits to wear for those very important meetings or when you have an important presentation to make.

A Well-Maintained Coif

As important as your outward image is—as it relates to your personal hygiene, skin and clothing—your hair is the finishing touch to polishing your outward image. Healthy hair is a must—a freshly maintained cut and color keeps you looking your absolute best. To maintain the look that is right for you, be realistic with what will work for you. Consider your hair type, texture, density, head shape, facial shape, neck-line and age, along with your ability to maintain the hairstyle at home.

Finding a good hair stylist or barber is as hard as finding a good dentist. You have to ask around and try different hair specialists until you find one that does a great job for you. Do your research, meet the stylist, communicate your desires, and always take photos of the looks with which you are most comfortable, that suit your personality and are easy for you to maintain. Include hair colors with variations of shades you like and don't like. There may be differences between the ideas of stylist and client, so providing photos will help to ensure that you are both on the same page.

". . . basic, beautiful, healthy, chic hair can be a reality for everyone. All it requires is some attention, the adjustment of a few details in our daily routines and a good stylist."

—Horst Rechelbacher, founder of Aveda and Intelligent Nutrients®

Now that you've found a good stylist, it is important that they create a maintenance plan that is best for your hair, understanding the balance between strength and moisture. This plays a major role in the overall health of your hair, for maintaining the cut, color and style. This plan is especially important for hair that may be limp, frizzy, brittle, spongy, weak or tangled. It is your stylist's job to suggest products that will work for your climate, your lifestyle, and specific hair/scalp conditions. Such products include dry scalp shampoos and clarifiers for product buildup, as well as swimming and sun protection products.

Avoid trendy or far-out hairstyles, and of course a ponytail is never appropriate for work. As an alternative, try a tamed pin-up or chignon.

For men, if you get your hair cut during your lunch break, please make sure you get it shampooed afterwards to keep from having hair all over your suit coat or the back of your shirt collar.

Helpful Tips for Improving Salon Visits

- Inquire about your stylist's training and knowledge.
- Establish a professional relationship and communicate your expectations to the stylist to ensure your satisfaction.
- Always tell your stylist about any likes, dislikes, challenges or concerns you may have.
- It is helpful to bring a picture of a desired look to guarantee your satisfaction.
- Make any special requests known when making your appointment.
- For special occasions, consult with your stylist to discuss your particular desires, and plan for a relaxed and comfortable day with no added stress.

• It is always beneficial to follow up at home with the hair care regimen recommended by the stylist.

Put Your Best Face Forward

A good haircut frames your face, so it is important to also have great skin. While this may seem like an odd topic for an etiquette book, consider that when a person looks tired, they also appear overworked. But when a person looks fresh and well-kept, they appear successful and vital, which is how you want to be perceived in your career.

Great skin begins with a healthy, well-cared-for body and is a reflection of your diet. When that is balanced properly, you will glow and your eyes will sparkle. In order to enhance your skin's quality, you must ensure you are receiving the proper nutrients. Protecting your skin is essential from the inside out.

Vitamins A, C, E and beta-carotene are antioxidants that provide protection from environmental damage. You can find these nutrients in yellow and orange fruits and vegetables, such as papaya, apricots, mangos, sweet potatoes, and carrots, along with leafy green vegetables like spinach.

The proper amount of water intake will keep your skin hydrated from within and supple. Eight glasses of eight ounces of water each a day is always recommended. You must also consider your body weight and activities to determine the correct amount of daily hydration. Many health experts suggest one ounce of water for every two pounds of body weight. For example, if you weigh 156 pounds, you would consume 78 ounces or 10 glasses of water daily, including any other non-alcoholic and caffeine-free beverages.

Understanding Your Skin

Skin is divided into two layers, the epidermis and the dermis. It is important to understand both.

The epidermis layer of the skin is made up of a substance called keratinized protein that protects your skin from weather, dryness and airborne bacteria.

The dermis is the inner layer of the skin and is where problem skin begins. The dermis forms the support system of the skin: oil, sweat glands, hair follicles, blood vessels and fat glands. The dermis is comprised mostly of collagen protein, which gives your skin elasticity by keeping it firm, well-toned and youthful-looking.

It is vital that you maintain a proper skin care regimen to protect and leave your skin radiant. Follow these recommendations for daily care:

- **Cleanse** to remove accumulated dirt, pollution or makeup.
- **Exfoliate** to remove dead surface skin cells.
- **Tone** to stimulate and tighten the face after the skin has been cleansed.
- **Moisturize** to bring balance and restore the skin's natural moisture.
- **Protect** to guard your skin from UV damage from the sun.

A daily skin care routine is beneficial but regular facial appointments are essential. An esthetician practices the healing art of skin care, treating certain skin conditions such as adult acne or blemishes.

Facials are very relaxing, putting your skin in a state to receive treatment. The results include very noticeable improvements in skin tone, texture and overall appearance of your skin. I recommend both men and women receive monthly facials.

Ladies: makeup is the last finishing touch after protective cream and a recommended necessity! At minimum, use translucent powder to take off the shine, neutral lip color to define lips, soft blush color to contour cheeks and mascara to brighten eyes.

Your professional image is a critical key to your success and is an important part of your executive etiquette. By giving attention to all aspects of your personal grooming—hair, skin care and how your clothing fits—you set a foundation for your professional presence that will allow you to flourish in every situation. Take what we have discussed here and apply the ideas that are currently missing from your presentation. You will find that you are looking better, getting out the door faster in the morning, and feeling more confident in every business situation because you know you are looking your very best.

VONETTA DUMAS
Diverse Images,
Image Design Consulting Group LLC

Diversity at its best;
When looking and feeling good
become effortless!

(202) 271-6972
vonetta@diverse-images.net
www.diverse-images.net

As a very passionate, talented and skillful Image Management Specialist, Vonetta Dumas enjoys making people look good and feel good about themselves. It's no wonder this Cincinnati native is changing the dynamics of image management. She now resides in the DC Metro area, where she founded her company in 2008.

She specializes in Total Image Makeovers for men and women in both their professional and personal lives, utilizing her 14 years of professional experience in the beauty industry. She is a graduate of Northern Kentucky University with a B.A. in Speech Communications and an A.S. in Business Management/Marketing from the University of Cincinnati.

Vonetta consistently improves her clients' confidence as a hairstylist, haberdasher and etiquette coach, teaching how to dress for function and fashion, how to maintain healthy tresses and the techniques needed to pull off a total image transformation. Her experience and professional repertoire have afforded her the opportunity to work with a wide range of clients, from celebrities to diplomats. She serves as a corporate workshop facilitator, does teen counseling for image and etiquette development and has been featured on *Fox News* as an "on-air" makeover expert.

Flawless Feasting

A Guide to Executive Table Manners

By Debra Gitto

In the mid-1800s, the English judge Lord William Stowell proclaimed, "A dinner lubricates business." This statement still holds true in the twenty-first century marketplace. A prerequisite to being a successful executive is the ability to foster and cultivate business relationships over a meal. Regardless of whether you dine in a refined dining atmosphere or a casual environment, manners at the table indicate your intelligence level, character and attentiveness to the finer details of life. And that translates into nonverbal messages about your professional competence and capabilities.

Yes, it's true that how you handle your napkin, hold your fork or communicate with a restaurant's staff can affect your career ambitions.

The importance of civility at the dining table has waned in recent decades. An American society that emphasizes busyness and activity overload has deprived younger generations, who are now in the current workforce, of the traditional family dinner experience. I have found that my young students eat their meals everywhere but at the table. Unfortunately, as they become young adults with college degrees in hand, they lack the basic life skills necessary to achieve their professional goals. As quoted in an October 2006 article in Business Week, Michael Morris, a professor of management at Columbia University Business School and leader of the school's Program on Social Intelligence, "Social intelligence is not a replacement for abstract intelligence. That gets you in the door, but social intelligence gets you to the top."

Interviewing for a job over a meal is commonplace in many industries, because it reveals the level of social competence of a potential candidate. Whether you are dining with a client, networking in the business community or attending a conference or meeting, the interaction is the focal point and the food is secondary. Croft M. Pentz, the author of *1001 Things Your Mother Told You*, published in 2001 by Tyndale House Publishers, says, "You can see how important manners are by watching people who don't have any." He also observes, "The test of good manners is being able to put up pleasantly with bad ones."

Taking Your Seat—Where Do I Sit?

> *"It isn't so much what's on the table that matters as what's on the chairs."*
>
> —W.S. Gilbert, English dramatist and librettist

Allow the host to direct the seating arrangements if there are no place cards. If the host does not offer guidance, take the seat nearest you. Honored guests are customarily seated to the right of the host during the meal. As you stand behind your chair, approach your seat from the right side. There is no gender distinction in a professional setting; a man is not expected to pull out a woman's chair. If he chooses to do so, however, a simple thank-you is in order. Handbags, cell phones, smart phones, briefcases and papers should be placed on the lap or under the chair, not on the dining table.

Napkin Know-How—Do I Blot or Dab?

History reveals that the napkin was once the size of a bath towel; this was before the introduction of eating utensils. This huge napkin was also utilized to carry home leftover food. When the host picks up her napkin, you may pick up yours. Unfold it on your lap, with the fold facing your waist. In the absence of a host, wait to pick up your napkin until two or three other guests have taken their seats. It is never appropriate to tuck the napkin in your collar or belt. It is best to blot or dab the mouth lightly when needed, not to use a sweeping motion across the mouth. Place the napkin on your chair when leaving the table momentarily, to indicate that you plan to return. At the conclusion of the meal, at the invitation of the host, loosely rest the napkin to the left side of the place setting.

Table-Setting Sense—Which Bread Plate is Mine?

I have experienced on many social and professional occasions the commandeering of my bread plate by a guest who may be lacking in the finer points of etiquette. In this situation, it is best not to draw attention to your neighbor's gaffe. Rather, kindly request another plate, or forgo the bread altogether. Your bread plate is located to the upper left of your place setting. Beverages will be at the upper right.

The place setting is a visual introduction to the meal, offering a sneak peek into the menu by the placement and number of silverware. The knives and spoons will be to your right and the forks to your left, with the exception of cocktail forks, which are also to your right. The dessert fork and spoon are sometimes placed horizontally at the top of the place setting, unless they accompany the dessert. As each course is served, choose the appropriate eating utensil farthest from the plate, working from the outside inward.

Styles of Eating—Do I Hold My Fork in My Right or Left Hand?

There are two styles of dining, American and Continental. For either style, you begin cutting your first bite holding your fork in your left hand and your knife in your right hand. The utensil handles are tucked in the palms of your hands, tines facing down, using your index fingers extended atop each utensil as leverage. In the proper American style, proceed by laying the knife at the upper right corner edge of the plate with the blade aiming toward the center and then rotate the left wrist outward and switch the fork to the right hand, holding it similar to a pencil, and raise the food to your mouth.

The Continental style, the most universally accepted style of eating, includes raising the food to your mouth with the fork in the left hand with tines down, eliminating the step of switching hands, as in the American style. The knife remains in the right hand during the duration of the meal and is utilized more in the eating process. Whatever style you prefer, just be sure not to hold your fork as though you were shoveling dirt. Or, as one anonymous writer advises, "It is coarse and ungraceful to throw food into the mouth as you would toss hay into the barn with a pitchfork."

Continental Style

When you need to sip your beverage or pause from eating for a moment, the American style dictates that your knife is placed at the upper right corner edge of your plate, with the blade aiming toward the center, and your fork is placed in a skewed position to the right. Visualizing the face of a clock, the handle should be resting at the four and the tines facing up pointing toward the ten, or, as it is traditionally referred to, the 10:20 position. In the Continental style, the knife and fork cross at the center of the plate, knife on the right, blade directed downward, with the fork tines facing down across the blade of the knife.

American Style

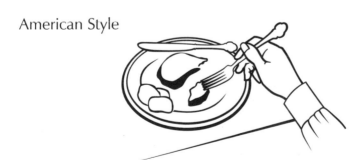

When you have concluded eating in the American style, the fork and knife are placed in the 10:20 position, with the fork below the knife and tines facing up. The finished position for the Continental style is similar to the American style with the exception that the tines of the fork face down. Whatever style you prefer, consistency is the key.

If soup is on the menu, be sure to handle the spoon similar to holding a pencil and spoon away from you, toward the outer edge of the bowl, where the soup has cooled enough to eat. A word of wisdom quoted from President George Washington's book, *Rules of Civility and Decent Behaviour,* most recently published in 2001 by Tyndale House Publishers, Inc., "…blow not your broth at the table but stay till it cools of itself."

Behavior at the Table—When Can I Start Eating?

It is appropriate to commence eating when the host begins. If you are seated at a banquet table, wait for two or three people to be served; wait until everyone is served at a smaller table of diners. Regardless of how ravenous you may be, maintaining your composure at the table reflects a positive professional image.

Even in a business dining setting, an upright posture at the table communicates self-assurance and authority. Keep your elbows close to your body while eating and resist the urge to rest them on the table, except between courses or after the meal. Your wrists may rest on the table's edge, one wrist in the American style, with the other hand on your lap, and two wrists in the Continental style.

Be aware of unconscious habits, such as talking with your utensils, touching your hair or face and fidgeting with your hands and feet. Avoid discussions about your health, diet, and controversial issues during a meal. It is fitting to perform nose-blowing in the nearest lavatory, and it is unfitting for a man to drape his tie over his shoulder, or for a woman to reapply her lipstick at the table. You do not want to be the first or last to finish your meal, so consume your food in small bites to be able to easily converse with the other diners.

Regarding eating with one's mouth full: in his book *1001 Things Your Mother Told You,* Croft M. Pentz quotes, "It's bad manners to talk when your mouth is full and your head is empty."

The Finger Bowl—Is This Dessert?

A celebrity co-host of a well-known talk show was invited to a White House dinner honoring the Queen of England. She was asked by a fellow diner, "What's for dessert?" In a moment of naiveté, she looked at the bowl in front of her that was filled with water and had the fragrance of roses, and responded, "This is it." Fortunately, the woman noticed another guest, former Secretary of State Condoleezza Rice, cleansing her fingers in the bowl, and realized this was actually not dessert.

The finger bowl was commonly used before the introduction of eating utensils. It is a rare occasion when the finger bowl appears today, and would typically be in a formal dining environment. Regardless of the dining situation, knowledge is power. Therefore, knowing the proper use of the finger bowl may perhaps save you from an awkward moment that reveals a lack of sophistication.

The finger bowl may arrive atop the dessert plate, accompanied by the dessert fork and spoon. In this case, place the fork and spoon on the table. Then lift the finger bowl and doily with both hands and place them to the upper left of the plate. When dessert is finished and the plate is removed, lift the finger bowl and doily with both hands and place them in front of you. Proceed to immerse the fingertips of one hand in the bowl, drying them with the napkin on your lap; repeat with the opposite hand. The finger bowl may also be presented after the dessert course has been finished.

Dining Dilemmas—Oops, I Dropped My Fork on the Floor!

We have all unexpectedly found ourselves in dining dilemma desperation—awkward or amusing moments when we would have preferred to crawl under the table than remain in our chairs. I will present a few tips to navigate through some of these common quandaries.

- Dropped silverware should remain on the floor. Quietly alert the wait staff immediately for a new utensil.

- Always sample everything that is served, unless you have a food allergy. In that case, a simple "No, thank you" will suffice.

- Remove foreign matter like gristle from your mouth with your thumb and index finger and place it on the edge of your plate.

- Point out to the wait staff, in a gracious manner, any strange objects in your food or on your plate.

- If a cough or sneeze comes on unexpectedly, turn your face toward your shoulder and cover your mouth with your napkin.

- If food is caught between your teeth, do not use a toothpick or your fingers to remove it at the table; excuse yourself and remove it privately.

- Remove spoiled food from your mouth by covering your mouth with one hand and remove the food with the other.

- If you have taken a bite of food that is too hot, quickly sip a cold beverage.

Eating Various Foods—Can I Eat French Fries with My Fingers?

- You can eat your french fries with your fingers only at McDonald's or other fast food restaurants. It is best to use your fork in most casual restaurants, and certainly in a fine dining atmosphere.

- Break off bite-size pieces of bread one at one time over the bread plate to avoid distributing crumbs on the table.

- Finger foods are fine, but be sure to have a napkin readily available.

- Chicken is eaten with the fingers only at a barbecue or family picnic.

- Use a fork to twirl only a few strands of pasta at a time.

- Be sure to taste your food before salting to avoid excessive seasoning.

- Shrimp served with the tails in a shrimp cocktail may be eaten with the fingers.

- The leaves of a whole artichoke are eaten with the fingers, and the artichoke heart with a knife and fork.

For more information on being an excellent host or guest at a business dining event, see Kay Stephan's chapter on *Entertaining With Polish and Pizzazz,* starting on page 87.

Mind Your Business by Minding Your Manners at the Table

Manners at the table, like all proper behavior, is an attitude of the heart that genuinely desires to convey the utmost respect and consideration to those around us, whether in a personal or a professional environment. As President George Washington wrote at the age of fourteen in his book, *Rules of Civility and Decent Behaviour,* "Every action done in company ought to be with some sign of respect to those that are present." Paul the Apostle wrote in the Bible, Philippians 2:3-4 (New International Version), "Let nothing be done through selfish ambition or conceit, but in humility consider others better than yourselves. Each of you should not only look to your own interests but to the interests of others." The traits of humility and a high regard for others communicate self-restraint and strength of character—positive qualities of a winning professional.

In the current global marketplace, people skills are as vital to a career as industry expertise. Since we could all use some professional polishing from time to time, arming yourself with the simple rules of proper dining etiquette will protect you from unexpected embarassing moments that could cost you credibility. Vince Lombardi, the late, great football coach of the Green Bay Packers, once said, "Confidence increases in direct proportion to preparation." Common sense, courtesy and applying basic etiquette guidelines are ingredients for a powerful, confident presence that will enable you to feast flawlessly as you climb up the corporate ladder of success.

DEBRA GITTO
Gitto Consulting

*Outclass the competition at every
opportunity in every way*

(609) 822-8164
dgitto@etiquetteinfo.com
www.etiquetteinfo.com

Debra Gitto is the president of Gitto Consulting, a premier provider of etiquette and protocol education, based in Ventnor City, New Jersey. She is in great demand as an instructor, speaker, and expert on the etiquette issues relevant to today's global marketplace. Her clients cover a range of industries including hospitality, law, real estate, healthcare, event planning and religious organizations.

Debra Gitto is a strong proponent for respect and civility in the next generation. She teaches social skills to students from elementary schools to colleges, is a former instructor for The First Tee, a national community-outreach program of the PGA and LPGA, and for the Young Plaza Ambassadors at The Plaza Hotel in New York City.

Prior to this, Debra was employed in retail sales and management. In an earlier career as a professional dancer she performed across the United States and abroad, sharing the same stage with Gene Kelly and Debbie Reynolds.

Debra Gitto is a graduate of The Protocol School of Washington® and is an active member of the Association of Image Consultants International.

Entertaining with Polish and Pizzazz

Being a Confident Host and a Gracious Guest

By Kay Stephan

Are you an average businessperson? Most people are average; but is that what you want for your career—average? How are you going to distinguish yourself from your competitors? One way is with impeccable manners. Effective entertaining is a significant business skill. Understanding the responsibilities and subtleties of being an outstanding host or guest can mean the difference between being perceived as average or outstanding. Remember that the purpose of business dining and entertaining is not the food; it is building rapport with colleagues and clients. Following these suggestions will allow you to elegantly maneuver through most situations. Let's get started with how to add polish and pizzazz to your entertaining endeavors.

Entertaining Preparation

There is a great deal more to hosting than you may realize, and preparation is the key to a successful social or business event.

When you extend an invitation as a host, be certain that the client understands that he or she will be your guest, and ensure that the selected time is convenient.

Don't say:

"Let's meet at the Diamond Grill."

Say:

"It would be my pleasure to treat you to dinner on Friday evening. Is that a convenient evening for you?"

Suggest a time and date before committing to a certain restaurant. If the guests accept, then find out if they have any special dietary needs: vegetarian, vegan, kosher or allergies. Now you are ready to select a restaurant.

If the host does not follow this sequence, as a guest, you can be forthcoming about your dietary needs.

If the host says:

"Let's meet at the Diamond Grill."

The guest says:

"I'd love to have dinner with you. Do you know if the Diamond Grill has vegetarian entrées?"

or

"Thank you. Is the Diamond Grill a seafood restaurant? I'm extremely allergic to shellfish."

Those simple sentences graciously inform the host of your dietary needs. As a host, pay special attention to guests' dietary and allergy issues, because this tells them you really care.

If you do a great deal of entertaining, it is wise to have several restaurants and servers who know you, your style and your requirements. Once you develop that rapport, you can be fairly certain that you will have no surprises. To add a bit of polish, have the server or maître d' swipe your credit card before the guests arrive; this is especially helpful for women who are entertaining men. You can verify the bill after the guests leave.

Entertaining at a Restaurant

As the host, inform the restaurant of the exact number of people attending. This requires RSVPs from your guests. If you are the host, arrive about 15 minutes before the designated time to make sure everything is in order. If you are a guest, be right on time. There is a French proverb that goes, "People count up the faults of those who keep them waiting." Being late is rude and could even be an inconvenience. Being "fashionably late" is not an option for restaurant dining and is unprofessional besides.

When hosting, wait for the guests in the foyer. The maître d' can escort the entire group to the table, with you bringing up the rear. Preplan the seating arrangement and show the guests where to sit; take your seat last. Whether you are the host or a guest, you may be seated if the restaurant foyer is not very large, but do not touch anything on the table. The table should look pristine when everyone arrives. As the host, stand as the guests arrive. If introductions are necessary, business protocol requires standing up to shake hands—this applies to both men and women.

Ordering and Conversation

Once the guests have settled and menus have been handed out, as the host, place your napkin on your lap. Everyone else then does the same. This may be the time when alcohol is ordered *(see the next section)*.

As a guest, you may want to ask for a recommendation as you consider the menu, so you can ascertain what price range is appropriate, since the host will be the last to order.

If the host says:
"The prime rib is excellent, and so is the salmon."

The guest is advised to:
Order something in the price range of those entrées.

If the host says:
"Oh, feel free to order anything you wish."

The guest is advised to:
Order a medium-priced meal with a salad and beverage.

Whether you are the host or a guest, ordering a shrimp cocktail, surf and turf, and crème brulée when everyone else orders an entrée and coffee, is the epitome of boorishness and naiveté. Remember—simple and conservative choices serve you better than overindulging.

The formal rule is to wait to discuss business until the end of the meal when coffee is served. However, in today's busy world, we may not always have the luxury of a leisurely meal. At least wait until after everyone has ordered before bringing up business topics.

Other Tips for Restaurants
For the host:

- In a fine dining establishment, do not ask for ketchup. It is an insult to the chef.

- Notice what each guest is ordering so that you could summon the server if something is wrong. For instance, if the guest ordered a well-done steak and it comes rare, you could ask the waiter to take it back and have it cooked some more.

- If you are at a buffet, be sure to ask the guests if they wish to make another trip to the buffet table.

- If you have time, ask guests if they would like anything else such as coffee, another drink or dessert.

For the guest:

- Ask for condiments at the time of ordering.

- Don't mention to anyone if food is not cooked to your taste. Eat what you can.

- During buffet dining, do not make your plate look like Mt. Everest. Remember moderation. Do not go back to the buffet unless your host invites you.

- Never order anything without being invited by your host.

For hosts and guests:

- Try to keep the same eating pace as others at the table—not too fast or too slow.

- It is okay not to eat every bite on your plate.

For more information on table manners, see Debra Gitto's chapter on *Flawless Feasting*, on page 75.

Alcohol

Now let's deal with the alcohol dilemma. First, you must respect your organization's alcohol policy. The days of the two-martini lunch are long gone. Many companies feel that consuming alcohol during business hours is inappropriate. During evening meals, alcohol can be acceptable and perhaps expected. However, that does not mean you are required to drink. Follow these suggestions to handle your alcohol questions:

- As a guest, don't order alcohol unless the host suggests it.
- If you are hosting and you want your guest to feel free to order an alcoholic beverage, then you order something as well.
- If you are the host and don't drink, ordering white wine and not drinking it solves this problem effectively.
- No one should feel obligated to drink. Whether you are the host or a guest, do not drink to the point of even slight impairment.
- Remember: conservatism and moderation are always a good idea for every business meal.

Ordering Wine

As a host, if you would like to order wine for the table, there are several options. You can always go with the old rule of white wine with white or light entrées, red wine with red entrées, or order a bottle of each. However, wine experts now recommend having a light-bodied wine with lighter foods and a more substantial-bodied wine with heavier foods. If you are not a wine authority, then ask your server—the wine steward, or in the finest restaurants, the sommelier—to make a suggestion. This is one reason why knowing your server is essential. If your budget is $50 for wine, you don't want the server to suggest a $500 bottle.

You could also ask your guests if anyone is a wine connoisseur. If so, let that person make suggestions and perform the "wine ritual." If you are a guest, be aware of the host's desired price range as you peruse the wine list.

The Wine Ritual

"Wine is bottled poetry."

—Robert Louis Stevenson, writer, essayist, poet

The following tips will help you navigate through most wine rituals. The well-known four S's will work—see, swirl, smell and sip. Here is more information to guide you:

1. When the wine steward brings the bottle, check the label to see that the wine actually is the brand and year you ordered.

2. The server will then open the bottle and may hand you the cork. Look at the cork to make sure the end is damp. If not, it could be an indication that the wine has not been stored correctly. After examining the cork, set it on the table.

3. Next, the server will pour a small amount of wine into a glass and hand it to you. Take the glass and gently swirl the wine. You are looking for wine clarity and want to be sure no cork is floating in the glass.

4. The wine novice may feel uncomfortable smelling the wine. If that is true for you, just hold the wine glass to your nose and try to notice if there is a "vinegary" smell. This could be a warning that the wine is spoiled. Wine enthusiasts will actually put their nose into the glass to smell and enjoy the bouquet of aromas.

5. The last step is to taste the wine to make sure that it is high quality. If it is, then you nod to the server, who will pour the wine for the guests. The host's glass will be filled last. While tasting, never reject a wine because you don't like it. Once opened, the only reason to return wine is if it has turned sour or vinegary.

Also remember that only the server or the host refills the wine glasses. As a guest, never pick up the bottle to refill any glasses, unless asked to do so by the host.

Toasting—Not Roasting

"A votre santé!" (France); *"Prosit!"* (Germany); *"Cin cin!"* (Italy)

A formal toast is meant to give tribute to someone at the gathering. The toast should always be positive and light. The duration of a toast can be only a few words and never more than a few minutes. Unless you are really experienced at toasting, it is best to plan what you are going to say; you don't want to ramble or make unfortunate jokes.

A convenient time to execute the toast is just before dessert. Champagne could be served, and everyone joins the ceremony, even with a glass of water. If you are the person presenting the toast, stand to give the tribute and then raise a glass to finish the toast. You may say "And here's to Valerie King, our person of the year." Next, everyone looks at the honoree, holds up a glass, nods, and perhaps says, "To Valerie." The honoree does not hold up a glass.

It is traditional for the honoree to stand, thank the toaster, and anyone else deemed necessary, and then say a few words. Then the honoree may raise a glass and say, "Here's to all of you who made this possible." This time, only the honoree lifts the glass.

Less formal toasts may be given at a business gathering to "seal the deal." In this situation, the toaster may remain seated, lift a glass and propose a toast to a "successful business relationship." The other people would then raise their glasses and nod or say, "Hear, hear."

Entertaining in a Home

Perhaps you wish to host a business gathering in your home. This is an excellent way to solidify and enhance your relationships. Here are a few tips to ensure a successful event:

The Invitation. Especially during the hectic holidays, send the invitation out at least four weeks in advance. Last-minute invitations can cause a disappointing turnout. Be clear about the type of event, the timing and any other details. Is it an open house, a cocktail party, a buffet dinner or a sit-down dinner? This clarifies the time elements for the guest. Make sure you are clear in your invitation that a spouse or one additional guest to an after-business-hours party is also invited. Ask for the ever-elusive RSVP with a "by when," as well as a phone number, or email address for responses. Include a stamped response card with a more formal invitation.

Planning a home event. Whether the event is catered or not, meticulously plan the food, timing and traffic-flow patterns so that guests are not confused about anything. Consider hiring some help for the evening, even for an informal gathering, to assist in the kitchen, pick up glasses, take coats and, of course clean up. This allows you as the host to be fully present for your guests and not stuck in the kitchen.

Being a guest at a home business event. Double-check the invitation. If the party is a sit-down dinner or a buffet, arrive at the designated time—no more than 10-15 minutes late. If the gathering is a cocktail party or open house, then you have more leeway with your arrival time. No matter what, do not arrive early to "help out" unless asked ahead of time. Showing up 15 minutes early can be very upsetting to the host, who is doing last-minute preparations.

Always bring some type of gift for the host to show your appreciation. Consider bringing candy, cookies, cake, wine or a personal gift, such as fancy soap or a picture frame. If you choose to bring a food or drink item, do not be offended if the gift is not used during the party. The host has made all the arrangements, and your gift may not fit the plan.

A plant or flowers is always appropriate. One caveat: If you bring flowers, bring them in a vase. It is rude to expect the host to dig around for a vase when other guests are present.

As the host, be sure to introduce everyone to everyone else for a small party or dinner party. Also, be sure to give some attention to each of your guests throughout the evening.

An excellent guest makes a point of having a conversation with everyone at the party. Be sure not to talk about work when spouses are there; doing so is rude and boring to the spouses.

Just as important as not being early is not being the last person to leave. When you see the party is winding down, take your leave, making sure you say goodbye and thank the host for a very enjoyable event.

The Corporate Cocktail Party

"I knew I was drunk. I felt sophisticated and couldn't pronounce it."

—Anonymous

The corporate cocktail party has been the downfall of many careers. Some people hate them; others relish the thought of free food and drink. Here are a few tips to make this outing an asset to your career and not a black mark on your corporate image.

Go to a party with the goal of meeting new people or getting to know better the people that are just acquaintances. You might aim to speak with at least five new people, using your best conversational skills. After you have met your goal, then feel free to enjoy the food, drink and your friends.

One thing you need to practice before attending any "stand-up" business event is to keep your right hand free to meet others. You don't want to juggle food or have a wet, cold handshake. The best advice is to have only a beverage or a small food plate in your left hand. However, with practice you can learn to handle both a plate and a glass in your left hand. Just like buffets, don't overindulge in food or drink. Getting tipsy or eating ferociously is a good way to sabotage your career.

Afterwards

Send a thank-you note after any event. A well-written note will make you stand out, since most businesspeople do not take the five minutes necessary to write a gracious thank-you. Many clients have asked if it is okay to send a thank-you note via email. Of course, an email is better than not sending anything, but you outclass your colleagues by sending a handwritten note.

To really stand out as a host, you can send notes thanking clients for taking time to dine with you.

These guidelines, which are not difficult, are the details of business entertaining that will make you more confident and your clients and colleagues more comfortable. It's definitely a win-win combination that will add polish and pizzazz to all your business and personal engagements.

Remember, being a great host and a great guest will never go out of style and will always put you on the high road to enhancing your professional relationships and ensuring your career success.

KAY STEPHAN
Professor Emeritus,
Certified Etiquette Trainer

Because manners matter!

(330) 854-3687
kaystephan@classicprotocol.com
www.classicprotocol.com

Kay Stephan, professor emeritus of Business Technology at the University of Akron, opened her etiquette training company, Classic Protocol, in Canal Fulton, Ohio in 2000. Since then she has traveled coast-to-coast providing etiquette training for businesses, professional organizations and university leadership programs. Armed with academic experience and primary research, Kay customizes programs to fit an organization's specific needs, which gives clients a competitive edge in today's challenging business environment.

Kay is the author of *Peak Performance for Office Professionals*, published by the Bureau of Education and Research in 2005 and 2006, and has written several chapters in academic books. She is known for presenting serious topics with a light touch. Her etiquette articles have been published in newspapers and magazines, and she has been extensively interviewed on radio and television, and offers an etiquette hotline through her email.

Kay's experience includes being the interim Public Relations Director at the National First Ladies Library and Museum, where she worked directly with Mary Regula, the wife of U.S. Congressman Ralph Regula from Ohio. She continues to volunteer for the library as a docent, representing former First Lady Lou Henry Hoover.

Seven Keys to Being an Accomplished Executive Leader

By Pamela Minyard, MS

As a certified etiquette consultant, and while building a leadership training institute that has taught hundreds of people how to become better leaders, I have come across many executives who are diligently seeking ways to improve their leadership skills. In this chapter, I will help you take your leadership as an executive to the next level. There are seven key characteristics of an effective leader, many of which you probably recognize in the mentors and role models you have admired and emulated during your life—or even recognize in yourself. These characteristics can best be defined as leadership skills. They are attributes possessed by leaders that make others feel comfortable with and confident in them.

It isn't enough to simply be able to identify these characteristics. Instead, one must be ready and willing to embrace, cultivate and practice them. If these skills do not come naturally, then a good leader must practice the requisite leadership strategies in order to become the most effective leader she or he can be.

"Leaders are made rather than born."

—Warren Bennis, Ph.D., American scholar, organizational consultant and author

This is great news for you, whether you are the chief executive officer of your organization or the executive secretary. No matter where you are, you can become a respected leader through your own efforts.

What makes an executive stand out from the crowd, whether she is leading thousands of people at a major corporation or a few people at a start-up? The answer is simple: Leadership. Executives who achieve major success have mastered some, if not all, of the leadership skills discussed in this chapter. Being successful in these areas is very important. If people see these characteristics in you, they are more inclined to respect you, listen to you and follow you. These skills build trust and confidence. Being strong in these seven areas will allow others to feel comfortable with being led by you, while at the same time allowing them the confidence to achieve their own personal potential, which will benefit your organization even more.

Key 1: Self-Confidence

The secret here is that if you don't believe in yourself, everything else falls by the wayside. I know a brilliant man who started moving up the executive ladder in international trade. He was charismatic; people loved him. However, because he did not have a college degree, he always felt one step behind his business colleagues. His lack of a degree had nothing to do with his abilities as a businessman, but his own diminished sense of self-worth because of this ill-perceived slight proved to be his downfall. Because of his natural business abilities, he landed a huge international contract with a foreign oil distributor. The day he was going to close the deal, he asked his best friend John to join him because John had a Ph.D. I think you can see where this story is going (especially if you are a fan of Shakespearean tragedies). John, using the man's lack of confidence against him, took over the deal. In short order, John cut the man out of the deal, and the man who had set out to make millions ended up barely getting by.

Now, this was an extreme case. Individuals sabotage themselves every day, even executive leaders, or people in line to become executive leaders. "I'm not smart enough." "I don't know how to do that." "I'm too young." "I'm too old." Self-confidence is a prerequisite for leadership. You cannot expect others to have confidence in you if you fail to have confidence in yourself. As a leader, you should have a healthy assessment of who you are and what you want to achieve. Note: I said "what" you want to achieve, not necessarily "how" it will be achieved. In his bestseller, *Emotional Intelligence*, published by Bantam Books in 1995, psychologist Daniel Goleman, Ph.D., calls this "self-awareness," or the ability to recognize your emotions—to know yourself—or better yet, to believe in yourself.

Even if you consider yourself confident, we can all use a little more. There are lots of ways to build your confidence. Success and accomplishment build confidence, like when you close a sale, have a successful first meeting with a client or effectively resolve an internal dispute. Even reminding yourself of other times when you have been successful—psychologists call it building on past successes—can build confidence.

Developing new physical skills like dancing, martial arts, or even yoga can give you a huge confidence boost. Developing your personal skills—like your public speaking ability, writing skills or communication skills—can be very confidence-building.

Also, when you can put yourself in new situations where there is not much at stake and succeed, this can be a great way to build confidence for more important tasks. For example, making a presentation to a few colleagues is a great way to build confidence before delivering a presentation at the stockholders' meeting.

Make an effort to boost your own confidence every day with this ritual. Stand in front of the mirror every morning and every evening. Look yourself directly in the eye and say out loud, "Wow, you are amazing! Great things are always happening for you!" This may seem a bit foolish, but it works wonders. Most people have 70 percent negative thoughts every day. This exercise can help you combat them. Try it for a month, and record all the amazing things that happen in your life as a result.

Self-confidence is not only expressed verbally, but nonverbally. Is your posture good? Do you keep your shoulders back? Are you slouching? Do you look directly at people? Are your hair, teeth and clothing in excellent shape? How you take care of yourself shows others how you will treat them. An image boost will definitely boost your confidence. Consult an image professional to gain many insights into upgrading your professional image.

Key 2: Enthusiasm

An enthusiastic executive is a leader around whom employees want to be, and she is a leader others want to work for. Think about how good you felt as a child when someone—a teacher, a parent, or a coach—enthusiastically acknowledged when you did something right or well. You were excited about the chance to do it again; you looked forward to another opportunity to succeed, to earn that enthusiastic praise—or vice versa. How did you feel when you worked hard at something and sufficiently completed the task—or did even better than that. Yet the reception you received from your mentor was lukewarm at best. How enthusiastic were you to apply yourself for that person the next time something was expected of you? Well, those same rules of enthusiasm still apply now that you are the one with the capacity to control the overall atmosphere.

Effective executive leaders are enthusiastic about what they do (their role), they are enthusiastic about their company's mission (the products or services) and about what they hope to achieve (their plan). They are genuinely enthusiastic about the efforts of their people and about the people themselves. Most importantly, they are enthusiastic about life and all the wonderful things their lives have allowed them to accomplish.

To be more enthusiastic every day, remind yourself first thing in the morning and again throughout the day why you are excited to be doing what you are doing. Remind yourself of all that you have to be grateful for, including your work and the wonderful people in your life. Plus, always remember to smile. As a leader, it is your job to check your enthusiasm level and make sure it is up. You want to convey that unstoppable internal energy that inspires people to follow your lead.

Key 3: Flexibility

As an executive, you are required to make decisions. Naturally, you want to make decisions that are in the best interest of your organization. However, your point of view may differ from others. Sometimes a leader may need to be willing to amend his course of action for the betterment of the organization. Consider this actual life-or-death scenario involving leaders who had to be flexible.

The casualties of American troops in Viet Nam were horrific. Poor decisions caused many men to lose their lives. In the military, an officer, usually a lieutenant, leads a squad or platoon of enlisted soldiers into battle. In Viet Nam, many lieutenants straight out of basic training and lacking combat experience were immediately placed in charge of platoons on the front lines of jungle warfare. It was at this moment that a lieutenant needed to learn about flexibility. Knowing the battle objective, he might eschew his formal training and instead, listen to the advice of enlisted corporals and sergeants in his platoon who had more combat experience and had managed to survive in the jungles of Viet Nam. If he had the flexibility to modify his own decision-making, the original battle objective could be accomplished, even if it ran counter to his formal training. The lieutenant who relied only on his own decision-making often led his troops through predictable maneuvers that inevitably cost lives, often including his own.

Obviously, as an executive leader in today's business world, it is unlikely you will ever have to face such drastic situations. However, one must remember that an organization's survival may definitely lie in your ability to be flexible in your decision-making.

Key 4: Supportive Communication

Good etiquette skills require the implementation of supportive communication in your daily life. This is a three-piece puzzle—listening, considering and speaking—in that order. Supportive communication is essential to building trust and respect between a leader and her followers. People prefer to have a leader with whom they can talk and who will listen to what they have to say. Strong executive leaders have the ability to approach a topic, even one about which they feel knowledgeable, with their ears and mind open. An effective leader listens to those around him, considers a course of action, how to explain his decision, makes the decision and then speaks.

Name those people in your own life who listen more than they talk. It is probably a pretty short list. How do you feel about those people personally? You probably like them, even enjoy being around them.

And when they do speak, you most likely listen and value what they have to share. Now name the people who talk more than they listen. This list probably contains many of the people you know. How do you feel about them? You may like some, dislike others, and feel indifferent toward most. How many do you truly respect and value their opinion? How many would you be willing to follow if they were in a position of leadership? Probably very few indeed. Consider one humbling thought. If those people were to create that same mental list, where would your name fall? Might it be in the "listen first" category?

Key 5: Self-Discipline

There is no "free ride" when it comes to polishing up your executive etiquette skills. Leadership is not a destination, but rather a journey. Self-discipline is about staying the course and working toward the goal. It is also very much about making decisions, saying no, even when it makes you unpopular, and taking great care of yourself so that you can take care of business.

As an executive, you can often feel pulled in every direction. Your BlackBerry® is ringing with umpteen messages, and you find yourself double-booked, with two appointments scheduled for the same time. The effective leader will evaluate what needs to be done, prioritize and delegate. This takes an inordinate amount of self-discipline.

Self-discipline does not come naturally but it can be cultivated. It does not take discipline to do something we enjoy. We participate in activities that we deem pleasurable with little need for self-discipline. Discipline becomes necessary when we encounter things we do not enjoy, such as working out or dieting. The same can be said for elements of leadership within an organization. For every task that you may enjoy as a leader, I guarantee there is an equally important task that you absolutely dread. For example, I love to network, to meet new people and tell them about my organization, but I do not enjoy balancing my budget. I love research and reading, but I dislike event planning. The effective executive leader has enough discipline to stay the course and manages to get everything done through the specific strategies discussed later in this chapter.

Key 6: Sense of Humor

You are hosting a dinner party for an important client. Just as you raise your wine glass for a toast, you sneeze, spilling red wine all over your navy suit and white shirt. The first thing you do, before running to get the club soda, is laugh. Note: be sure to finish the toast. I heard it said once, "If you do something embarrassing today that you know you will laugh about years from now, you may as well go ahead and laugh about it now. Why wait for years to pass?"

You can't take life too seriously! It is very important to be able to laugh at yourself. Being too serious can lead to stress and tension within an organization. Some people in leadership positions feel that showing joie de vivre will lead to lack of respect from their subordinates. This is certainly not true, unless you take humor to a level where it supersedes the overall goals of the organization, or you allow humor to dominate the established leader-follower relationship. Balance must be maintained. Don't put a whoopee cushion on a colleague's chair or tell off-color jokes. Leaders must show that they can have a good time accomplishing the goals of the organization and can enjoy being around those who follow their orders.

To enhance your funny bone, recognize that you may not be "naturally" funny and that is okay. Having a sense of humor does not necessarily mean you have to be funny; it means being able to appreciate things that are humorous, whether words, actions, or situations. If you want to be funnier than you are right now, take the time to study the art of humor. Enroll in an improvisation course at your local college, or watch a DVD of your favorite comedian. Laughter lightens a room.

Key 7: Be Ethical

People want to be led by leaders they trust. There are some business leaders whose ethics have been severely compromised. Stealing money from hard-working Americans may for some executives become more important than doing what is right, fair and just. These are extreme examples, but minding your ethics concerning every aspect of your leadership is very important. Even a hint of impropriety can set an organization back years. The executive who seeks to be honest and transparent, however, will earn solid trust from the employees, clients and the public.

As a leader, there are several ways you can model ethical behavior in the workplace.

- First and foremost, always tell the truth, even when there is a price to pay for it.
- Give credit where credit is due. Never take credit for someone else's work or idea.
- Praise people both publicly and privately.
- Admit when you are wrong.
- Be forthright with an apology when one is required.
- Make sure that your company's policies and procedures are upheld fairly and that everyone is held to the same standards.
- Keep staff informed about decisions that affect them and let them know why decisions were made even when those decisions may be unpopular.

The more ethical the leadership of a company, the more ethical the people working at a company will be.

Research suggests that technical skills only account for 15 percent of job and career advancement, while 85 percent is based on people skills. Incorporate and seek to master these seven quintessential leadership keys in your life, and look forward to enhancing your role as an executive leader every day of your career.

PAMELA MINYARD, MS
Pamela Minyard, Inc.

(914) 438-5627
pamela@pamelaminyard.com
www.pamelaminyard.com

Pamela Minyard is the founder and President of Pamela Minyard, Inc. a New York-based leadership and etiquette training agency. A highly sought after trainer and speaker, Pamela believes anyone can have the opportunity to be a leader.

She has run large and small leadership workshops and seminars for non-profit organizations and schools, as well as for corporate executives and small business owners. Her unique approach to leadership inspires all. She values helping others reach the next level.

Pamela is currently enrolled in the Doctoral Program in Executive Leadership at St. John Fisher College, New York. Pamela is also certified by two of the most prominent institutes in etiquette and protocol: Etiquette and Leadership Institute and The American School of Protocol. She was given the Inspiring Woman award by the WNBA New York Liberty in Madison Square Garden, New York in 2009 and awarded the prestigious Business Council of Westchester, New York, Rising Star "Top 40 under 40" in 2008.

Out of all the recognition she has received, Pamela's favorite "accomplishment" is being the proud wife of a high school English teacher and the mother of four well-mannered boys.

Leading With Finesse

By Katherine Bessell Wurzburg, AICI FLC

*"A good leader inspires others with confidence in him or her;
a great leader inspires them with confidence in themselves."*

—Chuck Gallozzi, personal development writer
and professional speaker

Are you someone who feels as if you were born to lead? I certainly didn't. One of my first experiences as a leader occurred when I was tapped for student government in my college days. It was a scary, humbling and ultimately, exhilarating experience. My first foray into leadership involved a very contentious issue that suddenly thrust me into the college limelight. I was a total novice in the ways of leadership and was lucky to be guided by a supportive and encouraging advisor—Jerry Varon—my first mentor. He saw something in me that I didn't, and was unselfish with his time and always positive in his encouragement of my efforts. I observed how he handled every situation, no matter how volatile, with finesse. Jerry's "win-win" approach to negotiating was an invaluable lesson that I was fortunate to learn at an early age. The end result was a positive policy change on campus that was very rewarding and stirred my interest in leadership.

The Finesse Factor

The best leaders use finesse in their dealings with people and situations. Finesse is a refined approach to leadership. It is the skillful handling and artful management of teams and people, whether volunteers, clients or employees. Finesse means using subtlety and tact in dealing with difficult situations. Subtlety is the key word here.

Having finesse means knowing how to make others feel comfortable and at ease during social interactions. Having finesse means responding to disagreement, conflict and anger in a measured and reasonable manner. Having finesse means maintaining confidences and speaking well of others. Having finesse means relating well to people of different races, ethnic groups and educational and socio-economic levels.

A leader who possessed and demonstrated finesse, and who was a great inspiration to me, was my late father, Harold Bessell, Ph.D. As a clinical psychologist, he was a recognized authority in the research and development of emotional maturity. In the 1960s he created "The Magic Circle," a popular developmental curriculum used in schools. Further research produced the *Bessell Measurement of Emotional Maturity Scales* (MEM Scales) and their application to parenting and romantic relationships. Dr. Bessell was the author of several highly acclaimed books, including *The Parent Book,* published in 1977 by Jalmar Press, and *The Love Test,* published in 1986 by Warner Books.

The most successful leaders are those who possess a high degree of emotional maturity, also referred to as emotional intelligence. Awareness, relating, competence and integrity are the four categories of life skills that define emotional maturity in the *Bessell MEM Scales.*

Interestingly, these life skills can be used to define the core competencies of leadership in organizations. Leading with finesse means possessing these four characteristics of effective leadership. Well-rounded leaders have strength in these four areas and a fifth I will introduce later. It does take more time and effort to lead with finesse, but the results are worth it.

Emotional Maturity

Emotional maturity, as defined by Dr. Bessell, means high behavioral functioning in the four important traits of awareness, relating, competence and integrity. More simply, it means good mental health.

Emotionally mature people are able to cope with life's problems and challenges. They are in touch with their own feelings and those of other people. They cope well in a wide variety of emotionally charged situations even when they are afraid, angry, frustrated or disappointed. They are in touch with reality and have good insight into their own motivation. In relating to others, mature people behave in positive and constructive ways. They care about the well-being of others and treat them with civility; that is, with consideration, respect and inclusion. They share decision-making and resolve conflicts constructively. They take initiative and responsibility for failure as well as success.

Because maturity comprises learned skills, emotional maturity can be acquired over one's lifetime. Some people are emotionally mature as teenagers. Others are emotionally immature throughout their entire lives, regardless of age. Some people have such low self-awareness that they can't recognize their own immaturity. These people seldom mature emotionally because they seldom seek help. They are quick to blame others for their problems and they cannot see deeply enough into themselves to recognize a need for change.

The most talented leaders understand the importance of emotional maturity and its relationship to the skills necessary to lead and motivate people. They know that growth in emotional maturity is a life-long journey that can best be achieved with conscious effort. They use this information as a tool to better understand their areas of strength and potential development. It is through self-evaluation that they build on their existing foundation of leadership abilities to further develop these skills. They know they will benefit from this growth personally as well as professionally.

You might be wondering how you measure up. Let's delve deeper into these four characteristics of awareness, relating, competence and integrity that contribute to leading with finesse and see how you do.

Awareness

Being an aware person helps you deal with people in constructive ways. It increases your chances of being successful in life and brings out the best in yourself and other people. There are two types of awareness: self-awareness (understanding your own behavior and its effect on others) and awareness of others (how they think, act, feel and respond). Both are equally important.

The most successful leaders typically are those with high levels of self-awareness. Often, leaders who encounter problems have low self-awareness about how their management style affects their employees and co-workers. It can be hard to step back and evaluate our own management style, but it is an important part of personal growth.

Self-awareness is also related to self-confidence, another important attribute of a leader. Building successful teams requires an ability to work with people who may be better at their job than you are at yours;

you must be able to guide and motivate them. I always try to surround myself with the most talented group of individuals possible. A confident leader is able to delegate to others, knowing that there is more than one way to do something, and that it is important to give others the opportunity to learn and grow. Self-confidence also allows people to admit to weakness and ask for help without feeling defensive or inadequate. Successful leaders are able to say, "This is not my strong area and I don't know what to do next for a successful outcome. Can you please advise me?"

Good leaders recognize the difference in behavioral styles of the people they work with and know that they need to vary the way they communicate with each of them. For example, when presenting policy changes to a group—such as the board of directors—it is important to understand that everyone approaches decision-making differently. Some people make instant, intuitive decisions. Others need time to digest information and analyze it before making a decision. Some want considerable facts and figures and will question everything presented. And some just want to know what the bottom line is. Being prepared for each of these styles will make the process go smoother.

Getting our desires and needs met constructively is an important part of life. Many people are uncomfortable asking for what they want or feel they deserve. Being self-aware means knowing the difference between being assertive and being aggressive. In nonprofit organizations, the best leaders find out what their members want to gain from their volunteer experience and help them achieve it. They understand that we lead busy lives and that volunteer hours are precious. People's time must be valued and their contributions must be appreciated. They need to receive enjoyment and fulfillment out of their volunteering, otherwise that will be the first activity cut.

While there are too many areas of awareness to cover here, one of the most important is accepting or taking responsibility when you are wrong, make a mistake or experience a failure. It is true that nobody is perfect. When you are unsuccessful, it is wiser and more mature to admit your limitations than to try to find a scapegoat. People will appreciate and respect you more if you show a reasonable degree of humility, objectivity and honesty. Saying "I was wrong" or "I messed up" is hard, but I can assure you that it gets easier each time. In fact, taking personal responsibility can be very empowering. Is there anything you have yet to take responsibility for?

Relating

Relating means being able to build rapport and good relationships with people. In our society, when meetings happen on the phone or online as often as they happen in person, developing skills in relating to others is increasingly important. While modern technology saves time, it also makes communication more challenging because emails can be easily misconstrued.

A good leader makes an effort to build community, socialize and create a real connection with their team. Knowing the value of building alliances, a good leader takes the time to personally connect with each team member and develop a relationship with them. Face-to-face is best, of course, but telephone calls or emails are valuable, too. Your efforts will lead you to rewarding professional relationships that will help you in your mission. Along the way, you can also develop important personal relationships and friendships that enhance your happiness. Many life-long friendships start through work or volunteer activities.

When leading a group or team, encourage each person's participation in the group effort, and let them know you are available for questions or concerns. A good leader has the ability to give, receive and ask for feedback—graciously.

A mature person is just as interested in the well-being of others as in his or her own well-being. Take the time to show you care about others by taking the initiative in showing interest. It can be as simple as asking someone how their weekend was, and acknowledging their response.

Good leaders work well with people, and can stimulate them to use all the abilities and experiences they possess. This can be achieved by establishing a climate in which free expression is encouraged. The leader then encourages participation and an exchange of ideas, but does not dominate the discussion. Leaders respect others' viewpoints and agree to disagree. They encourage sharing in decision-making.

Everyone likes to be appreciated for their contributions, and a good leader makes a point of recognizing others' work and contributions by taking the time to write an acknowledging note or email. A great leader takes it a step further and also informs others up and down the ladder of an individual's contribution.

Resolving conflicts constructively is a hallmark of a good leader. Disagreements are unavoidable, but don't need to lead to a major argument. Mature people are not so selfish or insecure that they need to have everything their way; rather, they strive for a reasonable compromise. The "win-win" negotiation strategy works well in solving conflicts.

I find an important part of relating as a leader is to be a cheerleader and encourager with colleagues, clients, board members and volunteers alike. When people feel happy and motivated around you, they are more engaged in whatever they are doing. How do you relate to the people around you? What have we discussed here that could improve your ability to relate?

Competence

To be effective, it is essential to believe in ourselves and to understand that our achievements are the result of our own efforts. As our accomplishments are recognized, appreciated and reinforced, we grow in self-confidence. Competence is the state of being an organized, focused, disciplined person who can solve problems effectively.

Being competent means applying energy and effort in constructive ways. It means keeping a positive attitude towards life's challenges.

As a leader, you set an example for others with your knowledge and abilities. Always be looking for opportunities to increase your competency, such as projects in new skill areas, degree programs, adult education classes, certification and individual research. Learning is a life-long challenge. The mature person wants to know more, to develop more skills and abilities. Be open to learning new things and sharing this knowledge with others.

Some other traits that demonstrate competence are taking initiative and rewarding others who initiate projects; being responsible by taking care of commitments without having to be reminded; showing high standards in the work that you do by taking the time to review letters and reports for grammatical and typographical errors; and being cooperative and flexible when working on projects with others. Being known as a team player is an important quality for leaders to have. Take a moment and ask yourself what you can do to be more competent in your career and as a leader.

Integrity

Having integrity means living in ethical ways. My favorite quote is from J. C. Watts, a former U.S. congressman, who said, "Character can be defined by doing what is right when nobody is looking."

Some of the key integrity traits are being truthful as honesty really is the best policy, being fair and not taking unfair advantage of people or situations, respecting property and the rights of others, not making messes for others to clean up, accepting responsibility when at fault and keeping confidences. Being a person of integrity is easy if you just follow the Golden Rule: Treat others as you would like to be treated.

The best leaders put their personal or professional agenda aside when it comes to decision-making for the organization. All decisions they make are based on one guiding principle: "What is best for the organization?" Check in with yourself. Is this your guiding principle for decision-making?

Civility

In addition to awareness, relating, competence and integrity I have one more key ingredient left to include in leading with finesse: civility. This is a hot topic in the media these days. There is a groundswell for more civil behavior in personal relationships, business and government. This "civility epidemic" was spearheaded by the Association of Image Consultants International (AICI), inspired by the work of Dr. P.M. Forni, co-founder of the Johns Hopkins Civility Project. Civility means using respect, restraint and responsibility in communications with others. Civility integrates the four traits of emotional maturity—awareness, relating, competence and integrity—in our interactions with others. It is also an important part of leading with finesse. How does civility play a role in your leadership?

Learning Leadership

If you are not currently enjoying a leadership role in your career and would like the opportunity to work on your leadership skills, start volunteering. Volunteering for professional and charitable associations is an investment of time and energy that pays great dividends by helping you develop skills, increase your visibility and positions you as a leader in your field. Through volunteering, you will work with people from a wide variety of backgrounds, nationalities, education and cultures. The diversity that volunteer organizations attract makes them the perfect environments to practice leading with finesse.

Whether you seek out a new role in a volunteer capacity, or practice leading with finesse where you are, recognize that leadership is a skill that is not developed overnight. It takes time, commitment—and as you have read—awareness, the ability to relate to others, competence, integrity and civility. Make a commitment to yourself and the people you serve to be a leader who accomplishes your objectives with finesse and watch yourself flourish.

KATHERINE BESSELL WURZBURG, AICI FLC
The Finesse Factor

(650) 949-3170
katherine@thefinessefactor.com
www.thefinessefactor.com

Katherine Wurzburg is a marketing expert and image consultant whose specialties include etiquette, event planning and leadership training. The daughter of an artist and a psychologist, she credits her upbringing with giving her the confidence, creativity and social skills needed to be an effective leader.

After working in publishing and advertising, Katherine started her own firm, Bessell Public Relations, specializing in the restaurant industry. After leading in her field, she changed direction and founded Designer Trunk Shows, providing her clients with garments and accessories from designer direct labels. She served as president of the Association of Image Consultants International (AICI) San Francisco chapter for two years and is finishing her fourth year on AICI's International Board as Vice President of Marketing.

In addition to professional associations, Katherine honed her leadership skills volunteering with nonprofit and educational organizations, including the Junior League, Stanford University Cantor Arts Center and the San Francisco Professional Food Society. She has won awards for leadership from the Junior League and AICI, and received the Outstanding Service Award from the International Foodservice Editorial Council.

Katherine is the co-author of *The Restaurateur's Easy Guide to Do-It-Yourself Public Relations* and the *Fundamentals of Leadership/Nominating Manual* for the Junior League of Palo Alto-Mid Peninsula.

The Etiquette of the Deal

By Linda Cain

By now you have probably discovered the importance of first impressions, dressing for success, and how to shake hands so that others will know you are friendly and sincere. You may have also learned the importance of knowing how to network, which paves the road for personal and professional achievement. Perhaps as important as knowing how to make a good first impression is to know how to make a lasting impression. Successful people lay out a plan that gets them noticed and sets them apart from others in their respective fields.

Whether you are in business for yourself or are climbing the corporate ladder, the following tips will help you perfect a business mindset while sharpening your executive etiquette skills.

Exhibit Basic Good Manners and Civility

Think fast and pay attention. Have you noticed that the world seems to be moving at a faster pace than ever before? We want instant gratification, everything to be ready immediately and our reports, updates or statistics delivered the minute we ask for them.

Forget about when you had to wait days for a response to your letter, or had to go in to the office to send a fax. Now we can send and receive information right from our cell phones, 24 hours a day, 7 days a week—even when we're on vacation or waiting in line.

Our connection to people has broadened, too. With access to social networking sites like Facebook, Twitter and MySpace, we can make and maintain connections with people from all aspects of our lives, all the time, all over the world. However, so much instant gratification is taking a toll on our ability to pay attention to the world around us. Sometimes we are moving so fast, we go through our days on autopilot. When that happens, we can hardly be at our best or really pay attention to other people. Yet it is only when we increase our awareness that we substantially improve the quality of our relationships.

At an event or a class, switch your attention from the technology to the people around you. In most cases, it is human relationships that will help you succeed, not your iPhone®, text messaging or webcam. I can attest to this and everyone who knows me knows that I LOVE my BlackBerry®!

Slow down and show respect. Pay attention to what people have to say, whether on the phone or in written correspondence, including email. Even if you think you know what the person is going to say, do not plan your answer before they finish. Once words have been said, it is difficult to take them back.

Email has the gift of instant communication. Remember: make sure to read the entire email before sending off a quick response. By writing about only one subject in each email, it is unlikely that you or the reader will overlook something important. And of course never use all capital letters, which is tantamount to yelling and is disrespectful.

Be kind and agreeable. In life and in business, conflict and disagreement are par for the course. You may have conflicts with co-workers, subordinates, managers—and yes, even clients. If you approach your business by putting others first, speaking with kindness and in agreeable tones, you will find that others will respond positively to you, mutual respect will quickly build, and conflict can always be dealt with fairly.

Keep on the sunny side. The best way to improve your reputation and advance your professional life is to make a conscious decision to be a happy, positive person.

A positive attitude is magnetic. People want to be around magnetic individuals, so you will attract friends, colleagues and clients effortlessly. Try these tools to develop and maintain a positive state of mind:

- Listen to inspiring music. For some, that's Springsteen, for some it's Shostakovich, for some it's gospel and for others, it's heavy metal. Whatever puts you in an open, happy mindset, listen to it!

- Breathe. When you feeling stress mounting, go outside and sit on a bench or a patch of grass, close your eyes and listen to the sounds around you. Whether it's birds singing or the hum of traffic, allow the sound to lift you out of any haze of stress and negativity.

- Write a daily gratitude list. Focusing on what you are grateful for and what's important in life surely makes you feel good.

Be a compliment giver. Being rewarded or praised for a job well done does good for both the giver and the receiver. We all love to be praised, although giving praise to others is often difficult. In business, compliments are simple ways of showing courtesy to others. When you receive a compliment, just sincerely say, "Thank you." There is no need to elaborate or seek further compliments or reciprocate. Simply accept it. At some future point, you may have the opportunity of returning the compliment.

Never give a compliment that is not deserved or is not sincere. Be specific. Keep the compliment focused on a job well done or a recent success. Find at least one person each day to gift with a compliment.

Listen first. If you perfect the ability to quiet your mind and listen when someone else is speaking, you will find that people will come to trust you and also, you will appreciate what they have to say. By listening to different perspectives, you open yourself to learning and may even find yourself entertaining new interests.

Develop a personal code of ethics. I believe that each of us has a responsibility, to ourselves and to those we come in contact with, to develop our own personal code of ethics. Just as our country is striving toward a higher expectation of accountability in corporate America and government, each of us should examine our own accountability.

". . . a code of personal ethics may involve being honest, showing respect, developing trust, having effective communication, being a good listener, accepting responsibility, keeping confidences, having a spirit of teamwork, setting and achieving personal goals, exhibiting high moral standards, reducing behaviors that reduce value, being kind, honoring diversity and fostering growth in others."

— *E2: Using the Power of Ethics and Etiquette in American Business,*
by Phyllis Davis, Entrepreneur Media, Inc., 2003

Our true character is revealed when we step up and are accountable for our actions. What are your beliefs? Take a look at your life—what does it say about you? Think about the people you come into contact with on a daily basis: is there room for improvement in these relationships?

Take the time to write down at least five standards that will help grow your integrity, strengthen your accountability and allow you to be recognized and rewarded.

Maintain the highest level of professionalism. To accomplish this, you must recognize that you are in service to others. So set the stage and prove your credibility in order to retain the trust of your clients. By treating others with respect and fairness, you create an environment where people want to do business with you.

Accept responsibility. Whatever you do in your strategy for success, always accept responsibility and never blame someone else. We are each responsible for our own actions and accountability. To point blame at others will only backfire and cause loss of respect. Our own self-esteem is reflected in how we deal with responsibility.

Handling Clients and Meetings

Your relationships with your clients, colleagues and others are vital to your success. Whether you are working in person with a client or from a virtual office, there are best practices that will support you in building and growing relationships.

Setting appointments. Always state your name, your title and your company's name, if appropriate. Be realistic about how much time you need for the appointment. If you set an appointment for 9 a.m., say that rather than saying "around nine," which may be interpreted that you are not serious about the person or the business. Similarly, when setting up telephone call appointments, be on the phone at the scheduled time. I also recommend that you set an end time for all appointments and calls. This way, there is accountability and it is clear that you value and respect the other person's time.

Be punctual. If you are going to an in-person meeting or participating in a meeting by phone, do not be late. Your time—and theirs—is precious and valuable. In today's fast-paced, highly technological culture, to be late is inexcusable and a definite deal-breaker. Set your clocks ten minutes ahead—that way, you will never be late.

If you must be late, call no later than five minutes prior to the appointment time and explain why you are running late. Even offer to reschedule the appointment, another indication that you respect the other person's time, but be wary of changing the appointment too many times; it may cause irreversible damage to your relationship with that person.

In the waiting room. Before you enter the lobby or reception area, take a moment to freshen up and check your appearance. Be sure your business cards are readily available, as well as any other materials you need for your meeting. When you arrive, hand your card to the receptionist and announce yourself. Decline any offer of beverages in the waiting room; you may, though, accept them once you are in the meeting space. You don't want to be juggling coffee and business cards, plus attempting to shake hands.

Until your contact walks in, sit patiently. Don't read, talk on your phone, text message or read email messages—these are all distractions. Just take the opportunity to breathe and go over your points for the meeting—again.

Set the stage. If you are the meeting host, it says a lot about you and that you value the person you are meeting with if you make arrangements to have their favorite soda, or flavored coffee or tea on hand. Always stage your meetings to create an atmosphere that will encourage productive business. If the meeting is to be in your messy office, consider using a conference room. If the meeting is to be at lunch or dinner, consider a restaurant that has a quiet atmosphere, conducive to conversation.

The main event. Once your meeting has begun, do not discuss your family, world affairs or the weather at length. Rather, after a sentence or two of small talk, get right to the point. Allow the other person to respond once you have stated your initial business, listen carefully, take notes and be prepared to summarize your meeting at the conclusion. Always respect and value time.

Always try to end on time. When you are nearing the allotted time for your meeting to end, it is appropriate either to ask permission to continue or to schedule an additional time to meet. Pay attention to body language and hints about whether the person may want to end the meeting, or schedule another meeting.

One of the most important things to remember is your follow-up. Be sure to write down any "to do's" from the meeting. Where appropriate, send a summary of the meeting to the client or host, indicating what was discussed and agreed upon.

Stay focused. Whether you are running the meeting or participating, stay focused and stick to the agenda. Cell phones should be turned off; your attention needs to be on the task at hand. Never rush a meeting, use harsh words or repeat yourself. Never take over the meeting and try to bring it back on track if it veers off track. You can say, however, "I hear that you have an interesting point, but can we table that until we finish with our current topic?" Works like a charm every time.

It is not enough in today's business arena to do only what absolutely has to be done. Successful people understand the importance of being in service to their clients, their staff and themselves. Typically, that makes us think of the relationship between the customer and the provider, but we are all providers and customers in our own domain. If we are stressed, overworked, underpaid and unappreciated, we will not provide the best service.

I have found in 20 years of working with large and small companies, nonprofit associations and high-level executives that having a service-focused attitude is key to a successful business mindset. Treating others with respect, putting their project or needs first and acting in a professional manner has earned me repeat business year after year and will do the same for you.

If you put your best foot forward, think of others, and answer when opportunity knocks, you will be successful. Know your own definition of success and take the time to equip yourself with the tools necessary to achieve it. Practice the etiquette of the deal. Stay centered and full of energy, keep a positive attitude, be considerate of others and be consistently passionate about what you do. You will exceed everyone's expectations—even your own.

LINDA CAIN
MCE International

Your passport to success

(626) 974-5429
lindacainoffice@aol.com
www.mce-international.com

Linda has been planning meetings, conferences and events for over 20 years. Her passion to serve others, and a love for the meeting industry, has given her an edge in the industry, resulting in her being a highly sought after independent planner. To enhance her meeting business, Linda completed her Certificate in Event Management and also became a Certified International Etiquette Consultant with the renowned Protocol School of Washington®.

Working with nonprofit associations, individuals and groups has been a rewarding experience and has allowed Linda to build a terrific team. Linda is lively and energetic, and her "do whatever it takes" attitude is contagious.

Based in Southern California, Linda incorporates her meeting skills and etiquette training to provide her clients with the most in professionalism, style and attention to detail. She owns her own company, MCE International, and is also a partner in Etiquette Survival, Inc., founded by Sue Fox (www.etiquettesurvival.com).

When not planning meetings or providing etiquette training, Linda loves spending time with her family, likes to read, and raises Pomeranians.

Cultivating Influence and Loyalty with Clients and Colleagues

By Dallas Teague Snider, CMP

"It doesn't take money to have class."

—Louise De Angelo Betancourt, my beloved grandmother

When you ask yourself, "How do I advance in my career?" or "How do I increase my visibility in the marketplace?" or perhaps, "How do I earn the business of a prospective client?", what you may really be asking is, how can you cultivate influence and loyalty with your clients and colleagues.

Until you honestly assess how you behave in business, you cannot get clarity about your unique gifts. It's common knowledge that people like to do business with people they know, like and trust. But usually we don't consciously think about why we like someone—we just do. We might give reasons like this: "Sally goes out of her way to make sure that I get what I need, and I can count on her to do what she says she will do."

In a world overflowing with corporate scandals, companies closing and the constant looming threat of downsizing, we are a culture starved for something reliable we can count on. Integrity, honesty and trust are the qualities we are all looking for in our careers. We can cultivate our careers through our professional relationships. The success of our relationships will have a major influence on the quality of our work lives, accomplishments or failings. This is why paying attention to your relationships is key in cultivating influence and loyalty.

Building relationships is much like making deposits and withdrawals from your bank account. When you make deposits into your bank account, there is a positive flow of energy. Money can flow without a challenge, because you have ensured that there is more money in the bank than you are withdrawing. If you are trying to withdraw funds from an account where there is not enough money, you will not meet your objective. The same principle holds true in your career. If you have not invested time and energy in a relationship, your phone calls may go unanswered, your requests may go unacknowledged, and the favors you need may be rebuffed.

Let's make every effort to cultivate influence and loyalty with our clients and colleagues. If you apply these concepts, you'll be well on your way.

Nurturing Your Professional Relationships

It has often been said that it is not who you know, but who knows you that allows you to meet your objectives. Etiquette is not about being stuffy and proper, but about how you make others feel; the same can be said for cultivating influence and loyalty. Think of the people you have met once who remember your name when they run into you at an event, or the co-worker who makes sure to let you know that there is a package waiting for you at the reception desk. What about the vendor who remembers that you love chocolate and do not drink? While he gives his other contacts at your company a bottle of wine at Christmas time, he always gives you a box of chocolates. In each of these cases, you could not help but appreciate the consideration.

Think of a garden. If plants and flowers are to grow well, they need love and attention. Turning over the soil often, adding mineral nutrients and careful watering all contribute to the healthy relationships that you want to nurture in your garden.

There are several ways to keep the relationships in your life well-tended. When they are healthy, you'll find a wealth of support and knowledge to help you achieve your personal and professional goals. If your goal is to build loyalty in a business relationship, often the loyalty blossoms when the personal relationship grows out of a solid business relationship.

Recently I was introduced to an attendee at a convention where I was presenting. "Oh, you're Dallas. Todd could not say enough about you. He told me I just had to take your session tomorrow," she remarked. I was pleasantly surprised and very grateful. I knew that Todd and I had developed a strong friendship through business over the past two years, but now he was acting as my champion and my advocate, telling others that I could be of value.

Todd and I have only seen one another five times, but our business relationship has developed extensively through phone calls and email.

In today's global marketplace, however, you cannot invite your colleagues in Nepal out to dinner if you live in Toronto. Going for drinks after work is out of the question if your clients reside on the opposite side of the country. Therefore it is important to look for ways to cultivate your long distance relationships as well.

Here are some ways to build loyalty and cultivate influence in your relationships, both professionally and personally.

Make a commitment to cultivating relationships. Relationships take time and commitment, so be willing to invest the time. When you do, you notice things such as when others are not well or need your help. Nonverbal cues develop over time. If you want friends, you have to learn to be a friend first. Be the one to make a personal gesture by sending a birthday card or recognizing your client's anniversary in some way. If your client received a special honor or achievement, sending them a note of congratulations is always a welcomed gesture. Last year, following an annual meeting for one of my clients, I sent the staff some foot cream, as a gesture related to how trying it can be being on your feet for four straight days, as they were at that event.

Show empathy. Empathy means being able to understand where a person is coming from and how they feel. Ask them about their day or how things are going with their families. Empathy doesn't judge another person, but accepts them for who they are. Remember the old saying, people don't care about how much you know until they know how much you care.

Empathy can be conveyed through active listening. See Terry Pithers' chapter, *Boosting Your Charisma Quotient,* on page 39, for more information on how to be a good active listener.

Communicate often. It is easier these days to lose touch. Still, you can keep in touch by cell phone, telephone, letter, texting and email, in addition to face-to-face meetings. Let the special people in your life know you haven't forgotten about them, even though the years and miles keep you apart.

Invest in someone's future. This could be as simple as offering a resource to fit a need. When you share your knowledge with friends and family, you are equipping them with a new, useful skill. You are investing in them—making a deposit. Mentoring someone is a great example. There was an advertising CEO that agreed to meet with a college student looking to enter the world of advertising and wanting some advice. Years later that same executive was competing for the business of a Fortune 500 company— against two more established agencies in the New York area. When developing their strategy the CEO thought, "We are a much smaller agency, but we will give it our best effort." Much to her surprise, they were awarded the account. A few months later the CEO inquired regarding the deciding factor. It seemed that the client was the father of the college student this CEO had helped so many years before. The client told her that he was looking for the opportunity when he could repay the favor.

Spend time with others. Always be inclusive. When you are going to a professional event like an association meeting or conference, consider which of your contacts might enjoy the event, and invite them to join you. Go out with business friends, and consider inviting people over to your home; this can lead to solid and rewarding relationships.

Relationships will wither away without proper care, just as flowers in a garden. Keeping a relationship going requires a commitment to share yourself with others.

Lagniappe Service

For all of my fellow Gulf Coast natives, the word "lagniappe," which is pronounced "lan-yap," needs no introduction. For those not familiar with this term, lagniappe means "a little something extra." I challenge you to adopt this concept as a rule of thumb in your professional and personal life. This is the ultimate key to cultivating relationships with clients and colleagues.

The little things *do* count. Think back to a time when someone spontaneously did a little extra or went out of their way to do something for you without expecting anything in return. A kind gesture, a compliment, or just a smile should not be overlooked. Something as simple as a handwritten note following a meeting sets one apart. I would venture to say this action made you feel important. You can engender this feeling in others by treating them with respect, dignity and honor.

How do you offer lagniappe-style service? Lagniappe is a mindset and a way of being. Shifting your complete focus to another individual generates feelings of confidence and trust. Once you establish trust, a relationship can begin to grow. Your personal "lagniappe" brand will be a platform that supports you throughout your career.

A hotel industry colleague shared with me a mistake that he regrets to this day. One day, he had to send a proposal to an important client who was an employee at a well-known overnight delivery service. The package was sent off by overnight express.

But the following day, the client called to complain that, although he did receive the package, it was delivered by his company's competitor! The hotel professional had not made the extra effort to send the package through the client's own company. This left an unflattering perception of a lack of conscientiousness. In fact, the client stated that had his boss received the package, the hotel would definitely not have won the business.

Be sure to check every aspect of your conduct to ensure your lagniappe service is sending the right message. Remember that in the corporate jungle, it is not the lions and tigers that will kill you—it's the mosquitoes.

Here's how you can use the concept of lagniappe service in two distinct business situations.

Lagniappe Service When You Receive a Visitor at Your Place of Business

- Prior to the meeting, turn off your cell phone and forward all calls so you will not be disturbed.

- Once your guest enters the room, close the door to avoid distractions.

- Pre-arrange the seating so you can sit corner-to-corner with your guest. Be sure that there are no barriers; unless, of course, you are still evaluating the relationship.

- When your guest arrives, offer a beverage such as coffee or tea. This shows hospitality. However, a savvy professional will graciously decline. An unfortunate spill would not enhance one's professional image.

- Initiate small talk and avoid anything potentially controversial.

- Be aware of body language; use mirroring to connect. Match the pace, word use, tone and inflection of the guest.

- Ask open-ended questions that will put your guest at ease and help build a better rapport.

- Maintain level-to-level seating or standing positions.

- Do not check email, sign documents, do any other office task or check your attire or grooming. Your guest should have your un-divided attention during the meeting.

Lagniappe Service When You Are Calling on a Client

- Before the meeting, go to the restroom to check attire and grooming, etc. Remember you only have a few seconds to make the best first impression.

- Greet the receptionist in a friendly manner and present your business card.

- While waiting in the reception area, be sure to move your briefcase or portfolio to your left hand, so you will be ready to shake hands.

- Graciously follow your host to the meeting room.

- Only bring in items that pertain to this particular meeting. Leave other materials in your car.

- Wait until your host is seated to sit down yourself.

- Business cards are generally exchanged before the meeting. Have them out to reference during the meeting. This is especially helpful when there are multiple participants.

The K.I.S.S. Method—Keep it Simply Savvy!

"Be faithful in small things because it is in them that your strength lies."

—Mother Teresa, Catholic nun, humanitarian,
Nobel Peace Prize recipient

Using the K.I.S.S. Method is essential in setting the groundwork for cultivating powerful relationships. Now that you have a general understanding of etiquette and protocol, you can learn some dos and don'ts to help you make your best impression. Remember that the perception camera is always rolling, and it only takes a few seconds to solidify that first impression.

It is crucial to have self-confidence and trust in your own business practices. By projecting a confident image right from the start, you can establish the groundwork for a mutually beneficial relationship.

The K.I.S.S. Method is a simple three-question checklist you can use for self-evaluation in any situation. To determine if your behavior is having a positive or negative impact on your personal brand, ask yourself:

- Does my behavior offend, insult, ignore or interrupt another person?

- Would I consider this behavior rude, awkward, unprofessional or tacky if I saw someone else doing it?

- Have I assessed the situation accurately to grasp the full implications of my actions?

Now that you have conducted the self-assessment, can you evaluate your strengths and limitations? The good news is that we can always improve our people skills. It is often said that knowledge is power, but before you can have knowledge, you must first be aware.

Congratulations, you are on your way!

Adopt a Servant Style of Leadership

"True leadership is when the people that know you the best, love and respect you the most."

—Dr. John Maxwell, leadership expert, speaker, author

When you think about the great leaders in recent history, who comes to mind? Perhaps Martin Luther King, Jr., Mother Teresa, or Abraham Lincoln. You may also include your mother and father, your first-grade teacher, or the bus driver who picked you up every Sunday so you could attend Vacation Bible School. What do these people have in common? They operated with a servant style of leadership.

The phrase "Servant Leadership" was coined by Robert K. Greenleaf in *The Servant as Leader,* an essay first published in 1970.

"The servant-leader is servant first . . . It begins with the natural feeling that one wants to serve, to serve first. Then conscious choice brings one to aspire to lead. That person is sharply different from one who is leader first; perhaps because of the need to assuage an unusual power drive or to acquire material possessions . . . The leader-first and the servant-first are two extreme types. Between them there are shadings and blends that are part of the infinite variety of human nature."

You can choose to adopt this philosophy of creating the desire to serve regardless of your current situation. Life is comprised of seasons, and we can adopt this concept at any season in our life.

Here are some additional thoughts to consider about embracing servant leadership:

- Invest in others. When you invest in others, you take time to learn about their desires and dreams and help them achieve their goals.
- Think "Serve First." This is another way to offer lagniappe service. What can you do to anticipate someone's need? How can you offer a little something extra?
- Give loyalty to get loyalty. You understand this unconditional bond if you have a dog or cat. Regardless of your mood, your pet still loves you.

When you put your attention on genuinely cultivating your professional relationships, you will find yourself surrounded by loyalty; you really do have influence with others. The best part of all is, you will find that when you serve others first, you too are served.

DALLAS TEAGUE SNIDER, CMP
The Impression Engineer

*Make your first impression
your best impression*

(205) 264-1361
dallas@makeyourbestimpression.com
www.makeyourbestimpression.com
www.businessetiquetteacademy.com

Dallas combines her passion for the business community with making a difference in the lives of others as an intelligent, high-energy speaker and trainer in the areas of business etiquette and international protocol. Author of *Professionally Polished: Business Etiquette Savvy for Today's Competitive Market,* published in 2009 by Tendril Press, she offers practical tools to help give those who want to recession-proof their career a competitive edge.

Formerly a twenty-year hospitality and hotel sales executive, Dallas founded Make Your Best Impression in 2007 to offer training in business etiquette, communications, and personal development. She is passionate about helping others be their best self, and eliminating the barriers that impede success through keynotes, workshops and personal coaching.

She encourages people to do the simple actions that are so important to building solid relationships with clients, business partners and peers. Dallas' warm personality and effervescent style inspire her clients and listeners to reach new levels of building sustainable relationships.

How to Say It and Not Regret It

By Barbara Khozam

Delivering bad news is never fun. If you want to be kind, as etiquette dictates, you may want to avoid difficult communication altogether, and that could be the downfall of your career. Know that this is a challenge for many. The most common concern I hear from managers, supervisors, executives and team members is, "How do I tell my people bad news without them getting defensive?"

Have you ever experienced a situation similar to the following scenario?

Supervisor Bob says to Cindy, "Hi, Cindy. Please come to my office in five minutes." Cindy immediately thinks, "Uh-oh, what did I do wrong? Am I going to be fired? How will I take care of my family? How will I pay my mortgage?" Supervisor Bob can't figure out why Cindy is so defensive when she enters his office.

Sadly, many supervisors, managers and executives don't understand why their people won't accept change or won't listen to negative feedback, and why they get so defensive. The solution is simple: these managers have never learned the tools of successful communication that top leaders know.

How do you communicate an idea involving change and get people to buy into it? How do you delegate tasks without appearing "bossy"? How do you give negative, or positive feedback? Regardless of your current level in your organization, the following information will help you communicate difficult information effectively.

First, let's acknowledge one of the problems with communication: attitude. If you go into a conversation with a negative attitude or thought, your tone, body language and message are also negative. Then your people respond negatively and you wonder why. To combat those negative thoughts, make a conscious effort to have more positive thoughts. When you assume the positive, everything changes: your face becomes brighter, your tone is more upbeat and your body language is confident. When you have a positive demeanor, the other person sees and hears a positive message. Then, hopefully, they will respond in kind. Of course, not everyone will be happy about your message, so the only thing you can control is your attitude and your delivery. Ensure that both are positive before communicating.

In today's business climate, three areas of communication are the most challenging: communicating change, delegating, and giving negative feedback.

How to Communicate Change

In our fast-paced business world, change is happening often. In fact, if your company is not changing, I would be worried. Companies must change due to competition, customer demands and new technology. If you are not open and ready for change, you are going to be very vulnerable. Your employees won't like change. Many have probably been doing the same job for a very long time. Change means they have to do something new, they have to step out of their comfort zone, and that's frightening. If you can't change how they respond to your message, you can change how you communicate it. The more positively the change is communicated, the faster people will accept it.

There are seven steps to effectively communicate change:

Step 1. State the change

Two things, at least, need to be communicated about the change: what and why. If your people don't know what change is happening, and why, they won't understand or buy into it. For example, one manager told me this is how he had explained a software change that was coming up in three months: "Hey, team, three months from today we're going to have a big software change. Okay? Great. So let's get going!"

What do you think happened? Sheer mayhem! If the supervisor had said, "Hey, team, three months from today we're going to have a big software change. In the long run, it will save us eight minutes per transaction, which equates to saving 200 minutes per week. Let's talk about it," what a different response he would most likely get.

Step 2. Listen to the feedback

If this change concept is new to your team, their first reaction will be disbelief: "No way! We just had a software change last year." This is a normal response. Hendrie Weisinger, Ph.D., writes in *Emotional Intelligence at Work,* published in 2000 by Jossey-Bass, that there are seven emotional states of change: disbelief, anger, yearning to turn back time, depression, acceptance, hope and positive activity. Since these are normal reactions, we must expect them and simply listen.

Step 3. Acknowledge the feedback

Sometimes people are immediately in denial, which is a normal emotional response. A great comment would be, "I understand you don't believe this is happening. It's true. Three months from today we really will be having that software change. Let's talk about it." Be careful about using the words "but" or "however" after the acknowledgment, because those words will negate what you are saying. Either pause or say "and." This is empathetic and lets your employees know that what they are feeling is normal.

Step 4. Maintain your emotions

The only person whose emotions you can control are yours. So make sure you are in a positive mindset before announcing the change to your team. Be rested, don't skip breakfast or your morning workout, and take a few minutes to get emotionally centered before delivering your message.

Step 5. Gain support

According to management studies, when a change idea is communicated to a team, 80 percent of the people on the team are neutral, 10 percent are positive, and 10 percent are negative. Of those three types of people, who is the first to voice their opinion? That's right, the negative ones. Then the neutral ones follow along, and now you have 90 percent against your idea. A better approach would be to talk to a positive person before the meeting. "Hey, positive person, I'm going to be presenting an idea today in the meeting that might be considered controversial. I just want you to give one or two supporting statements." When that happens, where do the neutral people go? That's right, to the positive. Now you have 90 percent for your idea and 10 percent against.

Also, if time and policy permits, another suggestion would be to have a positive person try out the change first, and then have them sell it to the rest of the team. There are two benefits: since the idea is coming from a peer, it's less threatening, and since they have already tried it out, they are reporting on a fact. They tell the good as well as the bad.

Step 6. Provide training and support

Of course you want to make sure your people are well-educated and ready for the change. Work together with your team to set up a training schedule. When you present your change idea, share how you will be supporting the change with training and other resources.

Step 7. Reward the acceptance

If you thank your people and reward their acceptance of this change, they are more likely to accept the next change.

Going through change is not easy. It can be made easier by our attitude and how we communicate before, during and after the process.

Once we communicate the change, we're probably going to have to delegate new or additional tasks.

How to Delegate Powerfully and Positively

All leaders, regardless of title, need to be good delegators. If they constantly come in early, stay late and do everything, they will certainly de-motivate their people. Here are three easy steps to delegation:

1. Be direct.

2. Be specific.

3. Tell why.

Many managers ask me, "Why do I have to tell them 'why'? It's their job to do what I tell them." Similar to communicating about change, without the why, it's hard for people to accept.

For example, let's say you need an employee to make 500 copies of a document for a meeting that starts in five minutes. Suppose you say, "Hi, Steve. Please make 500 copies of this document in five minutes." That was direct and specific. However, Steve is thinking, "Why do I have to make 500 copies in just five minutes?" or "The copy machine is over there; why can't he do it?" Without the reason, it's hard for him to understand. A better approach would be, "Hi, Steve. I'm going into a meeting with the CEO in five minutes, and I am still editing my PowerPoint presentation. Please make these 500 copies for me and bring them in when you are done. Thanks." Now that he knows the reason, he will probably gladly carry out the request.

This is true in so many situations. For example, let's say you have to make 500 copies for the CEO who is going into a meeting in five minutes. There are four people waiting in line at the copier. So you walk to the front of the line and say, "Excuse me, I need to cut in line and make 500 copies." What would they say? Probably something like, "Get to the back of the line." What was missing was the "why." If you had said, "Excuse me, the CEO is going into a meeting in five minutes. May I cut in line and make these 500 copies for him?" they will be more likely to say yes.

In the scenario at the beginning of this chapter, where Supervisor Bob asks Cindy to come to his office, what was missing? Yes, it was the "why." It's much better to say, "Cindy, I want to get your opinion on this project I'm working on. Please come in to my office in five minutes." Again, it's a very subtle change, yet very effective.

How to Give Constructive (Negative) Feedback

Inevitably, no matter how we communicate change or delegate, we will have to confront a non-performer. In my ten years of teaching seminars, I've yet to meet someone who enjoys giving negative feedback. And yet it's a necessary skill for any successful manager or executive leader. No matter how long you've been doing this, it never gets easier. You never know who is going to take it well, who is going to get angry and who is going to cry. The good news is that the approach described below can be used with anybody at any time. Do realize that you cannot control how people will react; you can only control your part of the conversation.

The following guidelines apply whether the feedback is positive or negative:

Be prepared. Before confronting someone, make sure you have the exact dates and times of any events, pertinent quotes and supporting documentation. The documentation will help you, and them, stay on track. I recommend that all leaders, regardless of company hierarchy, be very clear with their employees about their job description, policies, procedures, codes of conduct, expectations and consequences. Get their signatures on all documents. Ideally, that conversation would happen on the day they are hired, or on the first day you became a manager. This makes your job easier in that it takes the pressure off you and focuses on the documentation.

Focus on the behavior, not on the person. I would not say, "This morning you were an idiot and you were late." That identifies the person with his behavior. If I focus on the behavior, I would say, "This morning, when you arrived at 8:15 a.m. …."

Be specific. If the feedback is vague, it will have no meaning to the receiver and if it's negative, they will probably deny it. Be careful of words like "always" and "never." You need dates, times and quotes.

Manage emotions before confrontation. Similar to communicating about change, you need to be in control of your emotions before having this conversation.

Be timely. Although there is never "the perfect" time to confront someone, the rule of thumb is that it's got to be done within a 24-hour period. If you wait too long, the feedback loses its impact. For example, let's say you have a policy that your workers are supposed to start work no later than 8:00 a.m. Today, Suzie arrived at 8:15 a.m., so the best time to confront her is 8:16 a.m. If you don't confront her that day, she's thinking, "Cool, my boss didn't even notice." All the other employees think either, "Hey that's not fair," or "Hmmmm, nothing happened to her. I'm coming in at 9:00 a.m. tomorrow." Her late arrival can impact your entire team.

Public or private? Another question I get is "Should I confront the person in front of others?" The answer is, it depends on what kind of relationship you have with your team members and on your company policies and procedures. Here are four examples:

One manager, who had strong relationships with his team members and was a jolly man, would confront in public in the following manner. With a big smile on his face and in a very loud voice, he would say, "Hi, Suzie, great to see you here at 8:15 a.m. Hey, everybody, Suzie is here at 8:15 a.m. That's my Suzie, 8:15 a.m." as he would walk down the hall looking at his watch.

Another manager would say, with a serious look on her face, "Hi, Suzie. When you get your things together, please come into my office."

A third manager would simply send an email to Suzie, noting that she was late.

Another manager would sit in the late person's chair. When they arrived, she would stand up, look at her watch, and say, "Oh, hi, Suzie. Is everything ok?"

These are four different approaches—all very effective.

The problem with not confronting people in public is that if no one knows you did anything about it, they still have negative thoughts. So, again, it really depends on the individual, your team and your policies. When in doubt, confront in private. The constructive feedback formula is:

1. State the facts or observable behaviors. ("**When** you arrived in at 8:15 …")

2. Relate the impact to something ("**The impact is** everyone had to cover for you.")

3. State a possible positive reason ("**I understand that** there was a lot of traffic this morning.")

4. State the desired behavior ("**In the future,** I need you to call me first.")

5. Ask a confirming question ("**What do you think?**")

At this point, truly difficult people will argue and give excuses to justify their behavior; for example, "It only happened once." Your first instinct is to reply, "Once is enough." But a better response for each excuse is to go back to step number three and say, "I understand it only happened once, and …", before moving on to step 4.

Once the person agrees there is a problem, you can start talking about solutions. Great questions to ask would be either, "What are you going to do to get to work on time?" or, "How are you going to fix this?"

Depending on the severity of the nonperformance, you may add one more statement at the very end. "Great, and if this behavior happens again…" Use progressive disciplinary action—a verbal warning, a written warning or whatever your HR policy dictates.

You can use this formula on anybody at any time. If this is new territory for you, it may take a little practice on your part.

Now you are ready to tackle those difficult conversations!

Don't Procrastinate—Communicate

Communicating effectively and positively is your strategic advantage that will enable you to excel in your organization. Whether you're a manager or not, following these tips will make your message come across more positively. As a leader, go in with a positive attitude, stick to the facts, address issues in a timely manner and you will be more effective with everyone—especially your employees. They will view you as someone they respect, understand and trust. What more could you want?

BARBARA KHOZAM
Speaker, Trainer, Consultant

(619) 572-1117
barbara@barbarakhozam.com
www.barbarakhozam.com

Barbara Khozam is an international speaker and trainer who brings to her presentations a unique blend of humor and experience from both the business and professional sports worlds.

Since 1999, she has presented to over 800 audiences, spanning more than 35,000 people in seven countries. Whether working with multinational corporations or small businesses, Barbara tackles serious topics with humor and candor. In her down-to-earth presentations, she takes complex theories and applies them to everyday life and common situations.

Starting as a chemist with a B.S. in Chemistry from the University of Santa Clara in California, she excelled at her job but knew it wasn't her true purpose in life. Soon she joined a seminar company, and has been training, speaking, motivating and inspiring audiences ever since.

A lifelong athlete, Barbara Khozam incorporates energy, determination, and a sense of purpose in all activities. She played beach volleyball professionally for five years.

Press Protocol

Do It Like a Pro

By Holiday Johnson

In today's fast 24-hour media climate, it is more important than ever to strengthen your public relations (PR) skills through practice and preparation, and to know proper press protocol. We've all seen someone fumble responses to a reporter who has blindsided him with a trick question, or an interviewee on television, for example, who is clueless as to what the interview is actually about. As a communications professional, that's always painful to watch. What's worse, the exposure from that kind of interview negatively impacts your organization's public relations. It is my hope that you are never that vulnerable person described above. Whether you are an entrepreneur, a professional executive or new to management, public relations is an important component of your job.

When it comes to defining public relations, I agree with the definition of Moi Ali, a public relations practitioner based in Edinburgh, Scotland:

> *"PR comprises a set of practical skills and strategies designed to enhance the reputation of an organization, strengthen its relationships with key audiences and enable it to deal with crises from a position of strength. Public relations describes the way issues and messages are communicated between an organization and the public."*

The true purpose of PR is "to create a well-deserved public reputation versus cheap publicity—a reputation without substance," Moi Ali maintains. There are generally three "public" categories that we communicate with—internal, community and media (external). Because effective communication is essential to the success of any professional, your personal public relations wield a great deal of influence. I believe that PR is how we relate to the public in a genuine manner. This can have either a negative or a positive impact on our organizations and our professional relationships.

Media relations is one core component of the public relations triad. Over the next few pages, we will cover some of the principles of media protocol, focusing on interviews with the press.

First Steps

Before engaging the media, prepare to succeed by doing some fact-finding about the interview. I recommend getting answers to the five W's and an H—who, what, when, where, why, and how—before establishing a meeting date. Work closely with your public relations office or PR consultant to get these answers. Learn everything you can about the interview, such as:

- **Who** will interview you? Who is their audience? Who is your point of contact? What publication, company, or group is the reporter affiliated with?

- **What** is the topic or subject for discussion? What is the expectation? What kind of interview will you engage in? If you are being interviewed as part of a larger story, what is the slant of the story?

- **Where** will the interview air, or be in print? Where will the interview take place?

- **When** should you arrive for the interview? When will the interview take place? When will the interview air or be in print?

- **Why** is the press interested in you? Why is the press interested in the topic?

- **How** should you dress and appear? How long will the interview be?

I want to emphasize that preparation is a must for a successful interview. The more prepared you are, the more confident you will be in responding to the questions.

How to Be Effective with the Media

As a public relations and protocol professional, I have found that applying both areas of expertise is critical when engaging with the media. Next, we will discuss some guidelines to inform one of the external publics—the press or media.

Interviewing with the press can be a happy or a horrible experience. To avoid a horrible experience, let's go over some of the basic dos and don'ts during an interview, or when you are working with a reporter.

- **Do take every opportunity to share the story of your organization.** Remember the big picture. Your organization may have a mission or vision that impacts the community and the public. More people need to hear about what you are doing. People may not have heard of your organization and may be able to identify with an experience or a particular value that you talk about. Look to get your message out about the unique way your firm got started, or the community involvement your company is committed to, or a success story about something significant your firm did to help out a person or business.

- **Do prepare your message before the interview.** Your message should always be clear, truthful and said in accordance with your organization's values. Your public relations office or PR consultant can help you with this, so if you work for an organization, be sure to contact your communications office before you interview with the press.

- **Do be honest**—you never have to "spin" the truth. I had a client who wanted to "spin" information. Needless to say, I recommended against that idea. It proved best, because the reporter had all the facts before interviewing my client. We were able to confirm the information and inform the press of what was being done to improve the situation. Effective and genuine public relations educates and informs. The goal is not to cover up bad news, but rather to take responsibility if there is a problem and then to share how your company is fixing the problem.

- **Do follow up with responses in a timely manner.** More often than not, a reporter is on a deadline. Respond to follow-up questions or return promised information within a reasonable timeframe. Know that unless the story is about you or your organization, when a reporter calls you for a comment for a story they are working on, either about your industry or about a current event, they will often contact several people and use whoever gets back to them first.

- **Do know that the reporter does not have the final say.** A reporter's job is to get the information and write or tell the story from the facts they discover. Sometimes information comes from different sources, so everyone who was interviewed may not be quoted. The editor or producer decides on the final story and may edit the copy based on the space allotted and on what is most important.

- **Do be respectful.** Members of the press can be dealt with in a professional and civilized manner. In an "ambush" situation, you may be tempted to be rude to a hostile reporter, but just stay on message and keep your cool. Most cell phones nowadays have a video camera, and an unflattering video of you that shows up on YouTube® can ruin your career and your company's reputation.

- **Do establish a protocol, set boundaries and ground rules before the interview.** There should be internal or office protocol for working with the press. For example, almost all major government agencies have a communications office—generally internal protocol is for the press to contact that office to request an interview. Setting ground rules and boundaries is determined by an array of factors. Your public relations office or PR consultant can help organize this.

- **Do assume that everything you say will be broadcast or printed.** When giving an interview, whatever you say is "on the record." You and your communications person can draft questions the reporter may ask you during the interview. Practice your responses before the interview. You may know the subject matter well—it may even be part of your job on a daily basis. However, don't think that you can wing it or simplify the conversation, especially if you're dealing with bad news. Assuming that every question asked will be easy to answer is a set-up for failure. It is the reporter's job to ask questions—even the tough ones. Therefore, practice and preparation are a must.

- **Do use simple, understandable language that your audience will understand.** Avoid technical jargon, unless your audience is expert-specific. Since a news broadcast is usually watched by a general audience, it's best to speak in a universal language that communicates your message, avoiding industry jargon and acronyms. Recognize that most newspapers are written at a sixth-grade to eighth-grade level.

- **Do stay in your lane.** A reporter may ask you a question that you are not qualified to answer. It is okay to say so—then either offer to find out the answer, or direct them to a person who can respond knowledgeably.

- **Do get the facts straight.** If a reporter misquotes information, definitely set the record straight and give the correct information, based on your expertise and the facts.

Here are some things to avoid doing whenever you work with the press:

- **Don't assume that the reporter will finish your story.** Remember that you are the expert. The reporter is seeking your expertise on a particular subject. This topic may even be the reporter's beat. Don't let that deter you from telling the story from your particular vantage point.

- **Don't say "no comment."** The truth is, "no comment" is actually a loud comment! It appears to the reporter that you're hiding something. It is best to say you're not prepared to speak about a particular topic, or refer them to someone who can address their question.

- **Don't assume that you are the reporter's trusted buddy or that you can wing it.** A George Stephanopoulos interview with former British Prime Minister Tony Blair can look and sound like a casual conversation because Tony Blair has completed extensive media training, has many years of interview experience and prepared for the interview. Prepare your messaging or statements before the actual interview.

- **Don't ask for a copy of the interview for your records.** It is not common for a reporter to provide copies of interviews to interviewees. This would be like a work associate asking you for a copy of your mundane daily paperwork. It is best to ask when and where the article will be published, or when the interview will be aired. That way, you can secure a personal copy for yourself and your office records.

- **Don't assume the reporter knows nothing about your topic, or that you are the only source.** Depending on the type of story that is being covered, a good reporter understands how to get the necessary information. Before the interview, they usually have an angle and a lead.

- **Don't hide bad news, or cover up what seemingly is a bad story.** I've had clients worry about the press learning some internal information that doesn't put them in the best light. "The media can't find out about this," they'll say. If the information is really as bad as they think, more than likely, the media already knows about it. My response is usually, "What if they already know about it?" In my office we have an adage, "A bow doesn't make ugly pretty." Whenever it appears that the subject of bad news is attempting to cover it up, that news tends to stay in the media longer. So, always present information truthfully. As a communications advisor, my goal is for the organization to have a credible reputation over its lifetime.

- **Don't ask to see the article before it's published, unless to check technical facts.** If you are trying to convey a difficult subject to an audience, by all means offer to look the report over for technical accuracy, but not to scrutinize what has been written.

- **Don't say anything you don't want on the air or in print.** Take your time in responding to questions. Never keep talking just to fill space. Think about the question being asked. Know your message and include it in your response. Know that whatever you say may be in print or on the air with your name attached. Sound bites can go from 5-to-25 seconds, and quotes in a newspaper are usually one-to-three sentences.

- **Don't just answer yes or no.** The best response includes your message—with a fact. Remember the big picture.

- **Don't expect to win every time.** Sometimes you may get "bitten" by a reporter. Many of my clients are faith-based and more often than not a message may go against popular culture, but it is their message. I encourage you to remain true to your standards and your organization's belief system because taking a stand for your belief could mean the proclamation of an unpopular message, or being quoted out of context could lead to an unfavorable story. When this happens, it is a great opportunity to promote your message again.

Hosting a Press Conference

I have often been asked, "When is it appropriate to host a press conference, and what should I do as the host?" When it comes to press conferences, I give this advice: A press conference should be called if the information to be released will have a major impact on the public or on a particular community or industry, if you're getting a lot of inquiries about a subject or just to set the record straight about a hot story that has everyone talking. Nonetheless, press conferences are not for mere publicity. Smartly engaging the media in press conferences will enhance your organization's press protocol credibility. When holding a press conference, I recommend the following considerations.

Choose Who Will Be Involved in a Press Conference

Your organization's public relations professional or communication consultant should be the first person involved with planning such an event. Secondly, a buffer—typically your PR professional—introduces the speakers, sets and enforces the ground rules, makes sure the allotted conference time is honored and may address unanswered follow-up questions from the media. Include a spokesperson—it may be you— and subject matter experts who will address questions and speak to the topic of interest. Whoever speaks must communicate and articulate clearly and be the person who best represents the image of your organization. Keep in mind that "off-camera" communications from your staff who are assisting the press during the conference, are also representative of your organization. The messages communicated in print, as well as internally within your organization, must be consistent with what is being said publicly.

Prepare Your Press Conference Message

Have your messages prepared before the press conference. What is your message? All messaging is unique to the situation. However, there are themes like "safety" and "concern." Involve your communications professional to help develop specific messaging for your press conference. There are still reporters who respect the unbiased art of telling a story through objective journalism. Have your message reflect the truth about your organization with no spinning and no hype; this leads to your organization's long-term credibility.

Consider Your Nonverbals During a Press Conference

Pay attention to the nonverbal cues being sent from what you wear to the gestures you use; all of these elements help to impress your message on the public. Armed with this fact, remember to implement:

- **Good posture.** Most people shrink in height and put on a few pounds on-camera. So intentionally watch your posture during your press conference.

- **Eye contact.** In a press conference, speak to the crowd, not to the camera.

- **Voice projection.** Speak clearly, and use inflection with words when necessary. Avoid saying "ums" and "aahs," or other speech-fillers. I have a client who would say, "Praise the Lord!" after each statement. That was his speech-filler. The audience would walk away asking, "How many times did he say 'Praise the Lord'?"—and the message was lost. You can avoid speech-fillers by preparing your message early, speaking slowly and pausing before transitioning.

- **Effective gestures.** Whenever you speak, your hands can go on "auto-pilot," but during a press conference, be mindful to use your hands only when emphasizing a point. Excessive gesturing of any kind is distracting.

- **Conservative colors.** Stripes, plaids, herringbones and polka dots are not camera-friendly. Blues, grays and pastels look good on-camera. Avoid trendy looks, unless you're a fashion designer. Be remembered for your message. Fair or not, your clothing choice sends a message.

These tips can give you an edge when working with the press. However, specific guidelines must be crafted for your unique situation. Consider consulting your public relations office or find an expert who can advise you on press protocol and help you with a media and press strategy for your company. Attention to effective messaging and focusing on positive public relations with the media will go far to advance your organization and give it credibility with your clients, your community and the public at large. Apply what we have discussed here and next time you will be much better prepared when the media asks you for a comment.

HOLIDAY JOHNSON
M&J Communications

Communicating leadership

(202) 390-5900
request@holidayjohnson.com
www.holidayjohnson.com
www.mjc-com.com

Holiday Johnson has served as a U.S. Air Force public affairs officer, the media relations chief for Andrews Air Force Base, the home of Air Force One; as protocol officer to George W. Bush when he was President of the United States; and dealt with other heads of state and government officials at Andrews Air Force Base, Maryland. She has worked with national and international press luminaries such as Tom Brokaw, Tony Snow and Topper Shutt. With extensive experience in the communications field, she has earned numerous awards and recognitions in her career.

Holiday is a speaker, writer and coach for media etiquette. She is a member of the International Thespian Society, and has a B.A. in communications and psychology from the College of Notre Dame of Maryland. She is the principal and senior media trainer for M&J Communications, a public relations agency dedicated to advancing the Kingdom of God. She is also the founder of Ms Elegant, a company that provides enrichment and social development services to young people. Holiday resides in Fort Washington, Maryland, and enjoys acting in film and theater, water sports and good fellowship. She is also certified by the Etiquette and Leadership Institute to teach etiquette to young people.

Let's Talk

Your Guide to Effective Phone Etiquette

By Kim Maxwell

The ability to communicate via phone—both a land line telephone and cell phones—is a given in the 21st century. As vital as these communication links are to our personal and professional lives, we need specific guidelines for their usage in the office, out in public and everywhere else we use them. Yes, there really is proper etiquette and manners to practice regarding phones, cell phones and voicemail.

Instant messaging and text messaging are the ultimate in instant communication. They're just like talking on a phone call, except you're typing all your messages. However, remember that it is inappropriate to send instant or text messages if it will disturb those around you.

Just like in all other areas of our lives, learning and practicing proper etiquette and manners when you use these electronic devices has become a must. Etiquette and manners are essential to include at the top of everyone's list of skills, in order to ensure that we are all the best professionals we can be.

The Benefits

Always put your best foot forward when dealing with day-to-day business and work demands, including how you present yourself while

169

speaking with someone on the phone, your cell and the sometimes forgotten link—voicemail. If these rules of etiquette and manners are practiced throughout your company or place of business, you will:

- Distinguish yourself from the competition
- Develop and maintain business
- Build strong relationships
- Project a positive image
- Project confidence and authority
- Foster teamwork and collaboration

With the rapid growth in the use of email, cell phones, PDAs, voicemail, speaker phones, teleconferencing and facsimiles, it's more important than ever that all communication in a company be conducted on a professional level.

All businesses, regardless of size, should establish an electronic communications policy, including proper etiquette and manners, not only to set rules for employees to follow, but also to protect the company from possible litigation in the future.

Basic Phone Manners

Whether you are answering the phone or making phone calls, using proper etiquette is a must in order to maintain a certain level of professionalism, even when the person on the other end of the line is angry or upset.

- Always identify yourself when you make a phone call. Say your name instead of something like, "Hi, it's me."
- Speak in a pleasant tone of voice. Don't talk too loud or too soft.

- Learn to listen actively and without interrupting.

- Smile when you say "Hello," and while recording your personal greeting. Believe it or not, people can hear the smile in your voice.

- If you are placing the call, always ask the other person if this is a good time to talk. If it's not, ask when might be a convenient time to call back.

- Give the person on the other end of the line your full attention. Whether you are making or receiving a call, set aside whatever you are doing and focus on the conversation.

- If you find you have called a wrong number, first confirm that you have reached the wrong number by repeating the number, "Hello. Is this 865-5555?" and then politely apologize before hanging up.

- When visiting someone's office, always ask before you use his or her phone.

- When you place a call and someone answers the phone, do not say, "Who am I speaking with?" without first identifying yourself. Instead say, "Hello, this is _____. To whom am I speaking?"

- Always know and state the purpose of the communication. If it's an important call, you might want to practice a bit or make notes about what you want to say.

- If you told someone you would call at a certain time, call as promised. If you need to delay the conversation, call to postpone and reschedule; do not make the other person wait around for your call.

- Before you hang up, end the call on a positive and pleasant note, and say "Goodbye."

How to End Conversations Gracefully

There are several ways that you can end a long phone call without making up a story or sounding rude:

- Politely state the reason for ending the conversation: "I'd love to continue our conversation, but I have to leave for a meeting."

- Leave the conversation open, or promise to finish your discussion at another time.

- End on an "up" note. Tell the person how much you've enjoyed speaking with him or her.

As long as you are honest and polite with the other person, you shouldn't have any problems ending the phone call.

Voicemail Etiquette

Voicemail has many benefits and advantages when used properly. However, you should not hide behind voicemail. If callers constantly reach your voicemail instead of you, they will suspect that you are avoiding calls. Here are a few tips on voicemail greetings and responding to voicemail.

Voicemail Greetings

- Be sure to record your own personal greeting. Do not use the standard default greeting and do not have another person record your greeting. People already feel that the personal touch is missing because of voicemail. For instance, if a recorded female voice says, "Bob Jones is not available," the caller may not believe that you even listen to your voicemail messages.

- Write down what you want to say in your personal greeting and practice saying it a few times before recording.

- Always include your name and title or department, so that callers know they have reached the correct person.

- Your regular greeting should include your normal work hours. If you know that you will be on vacation for a few days or will be leaving the office early or will have different hours temporarily, record an alternate greeting to let callers know not to expect a callback for a few hours, or a few days.

- Try to keep your message as short as possible, but still include important details. If your message is rather long, you might consider stating the option to callers of pressing a specific number to bypass your message, so they can start recording a message to you.

Leaving a Voicemail Message

- Speak clearly and slowly.

- Be sure to say your name and phone number at the beginning and at the end of your message.

- Keep voicemail messages short and to the point. Do your best not to exceed 30 seconds.

- Remember that you want to make a good impression. Know what you want to say ahead of time.

- Leave the date and time you called.

- Let the person know the best time to call you back.

Taking a Phone Message

Always be prepared to take a message if the phone rings. A pen and message pad should be kept near each phone in your home or office for this very purpose.

Write clearly so the person for whom the message is intended can easily read it.

Always include the name of the caller, the date, the time and a number to call. I recommend repeating the message back to the caller in order to reconfirm all the information.

Telephone Protocol

Business telephones must be answered in a professional and pleasant manner.

- "Good morning, this is Susan Jones," or, "Good afternoon, Williams Marketing, how may I help you?"
- A caller should always identify themselves and their company's name.
- "This is Mark Gomez of Global Manufacturing in San Diego, California. May I speak to Mr. Mayer in your special projects department?"
- Give and take clear information: name, company, phone number and a convenient time to return a call.

Answering a Call

- Answer promptly, before the third ring if possible.
- Before picking up the receiver, discontinue any other conversation or activity—such as eating, chewing gum, laughing, or typing—that can be heard by the calling party.
- Speak clearly and distinctly in a pleasant tone of voice.
- Use the hold button when leaving the line so that the caller does not accidentally hear conversations being conducted nearby.
- When transferring a call, be sure to explain to the caller that you are doing so and where you are transferring them—in case they get disconnected.
- Remember that you may be the first and only contact a person may have with your company, and that first impression will stay with the caller long after the call is completed.
- If the caller has reached the wrong person or department, be courteous and try to help them find who they are looking for.

• When the called party is not in, the following responses should be used, both to protect the privacy of the person being called and to give a more tactful response:

DON'T SAY:	DO SAY:
"She's out."	"She is not in the office at the moment. Would you like to leave a message on her voicemail?"
"I don't know where he is."	"He has stepped out of the office. Would you like to leave a message on his voicemail?"
"He's in the men's room."	"He has stepped out of the office. Would you like to leave a message on his voicemail?"
"He hasn't come in yet."	"I expect him shortly. Would you like to leave a message on his voicemail?"
"She took the day off."	"She is out of the office for the day. Can someone else help you, or would you like her voicemail?"
"He doesn't want to be disturbed."	"He is unavailable at the moment. Would you like to leave a message on his voicemail?"
"She's busy."	"She is unavailable at the moment. Would you like to leave a message on her voicemail?"

Cell Phones

Although telephones are typically used in the office or at a place of business, cell phones are used more often in public, and therein lies the challenge. Today's technology can both ease and complicate our lives. While these devices are designed to connect us to important clients, co-workers, employees and vendors, we sometimes forget that we are not the only person in the room.

Cell phones can be a lifesaver in an emergency. However, they can also be a real nuisance to the people around you. Eighty-four percent of Americans have cell phones, and 48 percent of those feel they have to answer a call no matter what. Please let me assure you that the simple ringing of your cell phone does not mean you must answer it! Please wait for the appropriate time and place.

There are many places and occasions when it is simply inappropriate to take a call or a text message from someone. Remember that a cell phone conversation in a crowded area is not private, and that no one else wants to hear your conversation, or be walking behind you while you're talking or texting in an airport or crowded area, completely oblivious to other people.

Always turn off your cell phone in:
• Business meetings
• Elevators, or don't answer if it rings
• Churches
• Restaurants
• Theaters, concerts and museums
• Planes, on a bus or a train

- Carpools, unless it's okay with your fellow passengers

- Stores, or any establishment where there are people close by

- Sporting events, including your children's activities

- Line at the bank or at a fast food restaurant—actually, in line anywhere

In general, any time the use of your cell phone is going to disturb other people, either turn it off or move to a place where it won't disturb anyone. Always be respectful of those around you.

To practice good cell phone etiquette, put the ringer on vibrate or silent mode and let the call roll over to voicemail. If it's an important call, step outside or to a secluded area to return the call. If that's not possible and you must take the call, keep your voice low and the conversation brief. Let the caller know you'll get back to them soon.

It's rude to take a cell phone call on a date, or during a social engagement with others. It's also inconsiderate to take a call in the middle of a conversation. If the caller were present, he or she would likely wait to politely interrupt at a more appropriate time. Let the call roll over to voicemail and return it later.

Cell phone etiquette is just a matter of being considerate of others, which ends up paying off for everyone.

Even a basic cell phone model will allow you to correspond through text messaging. It's a simple, discreet way to answer someone, whether you're making plans for the evening or responding to a work-related issue.

You Are the Master of Your Cell Phone—Not Vice Versa

- If you really do need to take an expected call, let those around you know as soon as you arrive. If the call or text message comes through, quietly excuse yourself.

- Or, if you really must take the call, ask the people you are with, "Do you mind if I take this call?" and wait for their answer. Maybe they do mind.

- You can always tell the caller that you will call them back later at a more appropriate time or better yet, let the call go to voicemail and use a signal that vibrates to notify you that there is a message waiting.

Cell phone cameras. Think twice before whipping out that cell phone in locker rooms, at swimming pools, restrooms and other potentially compromising situations. Paris Hilton may not mind, but most of us aren't interested in finding pictures of ourselves on the Internet.

Handheld cell phone bans for all drivers. Currently five states—California, Connecticut, New Jersey, New York and Washington—plus the District of Columbia and the Virgin Islands prohibit all drivers from talking on handheld cell phones while driving. It is expected that more states and other countries will implement such a ban in the near future.

Ethical and Professional Text Messaging

When sending a text message, you may think that the message is only between you and the person you are texting, but actually your message may be far from private, given possible data retention practices of the providers and possible interception of your text messages by hackers. Bottom line—It's best never to send a hurtful or harmful message containing insults or gossip.

This all comes down to one thing—respect. Respect for yourself, and respect for others. The rules of proper etiquette and manners teach you what to do in different situations and what you can expect others to do. Being appropriate and professional when using phones of any kind, voicemail and text messaging will mean that these tools support you as an executive, instead of sabotaging you. Plus the people around you will appreciate your consideration, and that is good for your career, too.

KIM MAXWELL
The Etiquette Lady
Certified Corporate Etiquette and
International Protocol Consultant

(949) 443-4216
kim@theetiquettelady.net
www.theetiquettelady.net

Kim Maxwell is the founder of The Etiquette Lady, a company based in Laguna Niguel, California, specializing in business etiquette and protocol services for CEOs, presidents, corporate professionals and their employees. Kim says, "My workshops will give you the confidence to meet the challenges of today's competitive business world with sophistication, refinement, civility and poise."

Kim received her training and certification from the world-renowned Protocol School of Washington® in Washington D.C., a school known as the leader in etiquette and protocol services.

Kim says, "Everyone needs business savvy and the knowledge to establish themselves as a confident professional. Knowing how to behave in a business or social setting can make the difference between getting ahead or getting left behind."

Kim has appeared numerous times on KTLA Channel 5 Morning News, and writes a column for *The Orange County Register* called "Ask The Etiquette Lady."

Public Speaking with Ease

How to Captivate Your Audience

By Kristina Schwende, CEP

Whether you are planning to climb the corporate ladder, start your own business or raise money for a worthy cause, you will find yourself in situations that require that you present yourself and your ideas. Enhancing the impression you make and how you present yourself in every professional situation is the quintessential purpose of etiquette. This would not be a comprehensive book on executive etiquette without including a chapter on public speaking.

Unfortunately we have all seen articles stating that more people are afraid of public speaking than they are of death. For this reason most people avoid public speaking situations. Fear not, for knowledge is power and you are about to learn three simple and effective techniques to help you present like a pro every time.

Package Yourself with Professionalism

How much time do you think you have to make that critical first impression? Seven seconds—five seconds? Would you believe that judgment has already begun taking place the second someone looks at you? We begin to form opinions of others at a subconscious level without ever being aware of it. You might have a chance to change someone's perception of you if you are working with them over a long period of time. Even then, once an opinion is formed, it is very hard to change it. Before you run to shut the blinds, lock the door and live off the Internet, there is good news once you understand the process.

Your Appearance and Body Language

Environment. One of the first things you want to consider when planning your wardrobe is where you will be presenting and to whom. You want to ensure that you are not only relatable to your audience, but that you are also meeting their expectations. If you are presenting at a company retreat and everyone is in jeans, you will be out of place showing up in your suit and tie. On the other hand, if you are presenting at a conference and your audience is wearing business attire and you show up in a shirt and jeans you will lose credibility with your audience. You will have to work harder to earn their respect and attention, and some of your audience will not get past the fact that you are dressed inappropriately.

Expectations. People may have certain expectations of you based on your profession. For example, if you are a lawyer or accountant and they are hiring you for your expertise, you will most likely be expected to dress the part. Sometimes people will dress up when meeting you for the first time, but normally they are rather informal. When it comes time to present to their group, you could make your audience feel uncomfortable if you show up overdressed. Don't be shy about asking what their expectations or preferences are. Most people will appreciate your consideration. Normally, though, it is always better to start out high on the professional scale than the other way around.

Professional business attire. There are basic rules that apply to both men and women when it comes to putting together a professional look.

Just remember the words classic and conservative and apply them as follows:

- Darker colors are more formal, with black being the most formal—especially when combined with a well-made white shirt/blouse.

- Solid colors are more professional than prints or tweeds.

- Shoes should always be clean, polished and in good condition. Believe me, people will notice if your shoes are scuffed. Especially if they are looking up at you on a stage or platform.

- Accessories can make or break your overall look. Piercings are very common, but I recommend caution. Men should not wear any piercings and women should keep it to one piercing in each ear. Dangly earrings will be a distraction and should be avoided, as should bracelets that make a noise when you move. Keep rings to the ring finger only and try to avoid anything big and trendy.

Walking Styles

There is an unforgettable scene from the 1996 Metro-Goldwyn-Mayer movie, The Bird Cage, where Robin Williams is trying to teach Nathan Lane to walk like John Wayne so that he can come across as more masculine. While I am not suggesting that you learn to walk like John Wayne, I am suggesting you take note of your walking style and that of the people around you. Do they look confident, timid or angry? Have you noticed that many people shuffle their feet when they walk? This seems to be another trend and one I suggest eradicating from your personal style, as it will make you appear lazy and child-like.

Posture

It is amazing how something as simple as standing up straight and pulling your shoulders back can have such a dramatic effect on your appearance. In the blink of an eye, you have grown two inches, suddenly appear more confident and alive and it did not cost you a dime. I thank my mother every chance I get for all those years of telling me to "Sit up straight", "Stand up straight", and "Pull your shoulders back." Also, be sure to stay away from disempowering stances such as clasping your hands together in front of you, shifting your body weight from one foot to the other, continually looking at the floor, etc. These all rob you of your power and credibility.

For Women

Let's talk about the unique challenges facing women in business today. Surprisingly, they have not changed very much over the years. Did you know that in 2008, only three percent of CEOs of Fortune 500 companies were women, and women held only 15 percent of positions on boards of directors?

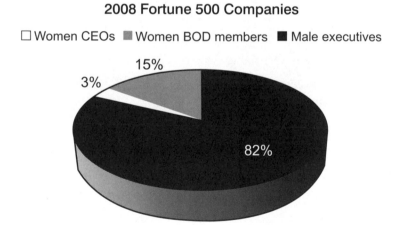

2008 Fortune 500 Companies

☐ Women CEOs ◼ Women BOD members ◼ Male executives

Source: The Whitehouse Project, 2008 Report Executive Summary

Certainly, some of this is due to the choices made around work/life balance. Unfortunately, some is also due to the way women present themselves in business. I find it very distressing to see so many businesswomen dressed as though they are heading out for the company picnic while their male counterparts are in business suits and ties. I see this often when watching the news—the man looking very professional in a suit and his female colleague in a dressy T-shirt and slacks or a skirt. Why put yourself at a disadvantage? Remember, the goal is to create a look that allows people to hear what you have to say in a professional and credible manner.

Using Subtle Cues Effectively

Speech patterns. Remember that 38 percent of someone's impression of you comes from your vocal tone, pace and inflection. My son is 20 years old and I have always done my best to set the example for him—or so I thought. Imagine my horror when I realized that I had begun speaking more like him instead of vice versa. I noticed that I was ending my sentences on an up note—almost like a question. I then began noticing how many people speak this way—not just my son and his friends, but people in business situations.

I highly encourage you to pay close attention to this disturbing phenomenon and stop it in its tracks. It is a very immature speech pattern, which is adorable in young children but a credibility killer in adults.

It is also important to watch your overall tone of voice, using different tones as appropriate. In terms of pacing, it is a good idea to vary your pacing for the best effect.

The words we use. These only count for seven percent of your first impression. However, do make sure you are using appropriate language for your audience and don't be too casual, as in this example. There was a business partner I had been dealing with over a period of months. He was very personable, impeccably dressed and highly professional. Then one day we were joking about something and he used the *F* word. My opinion of him immediately dropped down considerably. It can be very easy to become casual with our vocabulary, especially as we become more comfortable around people. I am also aware that many people do use, shall we say, colorful language in business. I would ask that you raise yourself to a higher standard. As the saying goes: "It's hard to soar like an eagle when you're surrounded by turkeys." Be the eagle and soar proudly.

Engaging Your Audience

There are generally three situations that require you to speak in front of people:

You are the speaker. You are brought in as a speaker to share information, and there is no opportunity for people to ask questions. This is probably the most popular option for the presenter but not the audience. You will often see this with very large audiences or other situations where asking questions is just not feasible. It gets the speaker off the hook but can leave the audience feeling frustrated unless you make yourself available after the session to meet with people.

You are teaching or presenting. You are teaching a course or presenting information where people are encouraged to ask questions. This is a more common scenario where you are presenting information and looking for questions/feedback from your audience. This puts the presenter in the spotlight and can be unnerving for the unprepared.

Facilitating. You are facilitating a session where you are expected to not only answer questions but also be the conductor and mediator—all rolled into one. The role of the facilitator can be very gratifying as you truly have complete control of the session. You are responsible for bringing people through a process, helping them to achieve their desired goals, and even being the referee when needed.

Ways to Interact with Your Audience

There is something magical when you connect with your audience; when you see their eyes light up as they grasp a concept and you get to share in their excitement. Let's look at a few ways to help you facilitate a strong connection:

- **Greet them as they come in.** Have you ever been to a meeting or presentation where you were greeted by the speaker? Some speakers do this but many do not. It is a wonderful way to make a great first impression and start the connection process.

- **Set the context.** Can you imagine trying to learn a sport without any rules? Running a successful meeting or presentation is no different. That is where setting the context (the rules) comes in to play. Rather than doing it yourself, allow your audience to decide what the rules should be. You can guide them in the right direction by listing various issues that could arise such as cell phones going off, people arriving late, disagreements, etc. Write down the agreed rules on a flipchart and post them on the wall for easy reference.

- **Start with a question or story.** Instead of starting off by talking about yourself, ask compelling questions or tell a great story related to your topic.

- **Exercises.** Make sure you have exercises to help cement the learning objective for each topic. Exercises can be verbal, written, individual or in groups. Shake it up. Get people moving around, interacting with each other and with you.

- **Sharing.** Ask people to share their learning after each exercise. This gives you an opportunity to see if you are doing your job properly and gives them a chance to shine in the spotlight. Remember to applaud people after they share, as this validates their contribution and effort.

The scenarios and strategies are almost endless, which is why there are so many books on the subject. I recommend that you continue your learning through books and/or courses.

Dealing with Challenges from the Audience

While working with an excited, cooperative audience is exhilarating, dealing with difficult personalities can be—well—difficult. Equip yourself to deal with these audience members.

- **The know-it-all.** This person likes to think they know more than you and can't wait to share their expertise with the room. Do not allow this person to take over the session. Acknowledge their expertise and thank them for sharing. Then, move to the opposite side of the room and ask others to share their thoughts. If they continue to try to grab the spotlight, speak to them at the break. Again, thank them for their expertise but tell them that you are concerned that others may not have the chance to participate as well. You could also get them involved by asking them to write down audience ideas on a flipchart.

- **The debater.** This person usually has a personal agenda and wants to undermine your credibility. Do not allow yourself to be sucked in to the debate. Acknowledge their question and then bring others in to the discussion to get their opinion. If they continue to pursue the debate, acknowledge their concern and offer to address it at the break.

- **The latecomer.** Some people arrive late through circumstances beyond their control, while others are chronically late. If someone arrives late, stop speaking, acknowledge their presence and either give them a brief overview of what you have covered or have them pair up with someone at their table. If they arrive late again, stop talking, acknowledge their presence and then refer to the agreed rules that deal with late arrivals.

• **The reluctant or shy person.** I do not recommend calling on people who obviously do not want to participate, as this could be quite embarrassing for them. This is where working in groups is key, ensuring that each person at the table has a role to play. I would also check in with them at the break to see what needs to happen in order for them to feel comfortable participating.

• **Escalating disturbances.** There may be times that you will have to ask someone to leave; otherwise, you do not have any hope of carrying on with your presentation. If necessary, call an early break—most people won't mind—and confront the person's behavior in a non-aggressive but assertive manner. Acknowledge the problem and ask what needs to happen in order for them to move forward. If they continue to be negative, argumentative, rude, etc., then ask them to leave. In a public program situation where they have paid a fee I suggest offering to refund their money.

Final Tips

The last thing you want to do is walk into a presentation without doing any preparation or rehearsing. Many people think that just because they know their material inside and out, they can go in and "wing it." Or, they do all the preparation and assume that going over their presentation in their mind is enough practice. I guarantee that the way it sounds in your head is dramatically different from how it will sound coming out of your mouth.

Do you find yourself getting nervous? Everyone gets nervous. Zig Ziglar, one of the greatest public speakers of our time, once said that even after all his years of public speaking he still got butterflies in his stomach before going on stage. He also said that the day he stopped feeling this way was the day he would stop presenting. Why would he say that? Because that feeling gave him the edge he needed to be his best. Here are some tips to help you with your butterflies:

- The next time you are feeling nervous, tell yourself you are excited.

- Take the focus off yourself and put it on your audience. Make good eye contact and create that connection.

- Do some light exercise, but be careful with this as you do not want to get on stage all sweaty and out of breath.

- Do some meditation and/or deep breathing.

- Practice, practice and then practice some more! The more comfortable you are with your material, the less nervous you will feel.

- Videotape yourself presenting and review it. If you do not have a video camera, practice in front of a mirror. I would highly recommend recording yourself as well and listen to this over and over again.

Remember, you know more than your audience does. They will not notice if you forget to say something. Making mistakes will not kill you! They are what make you better. By continually learning and practicing your craft, you can become the polished speaker you desire to be.

KRISTINA SCHWENDE, CEP
Sabre Business Skills

(778) 371-1543 x 201
kschwende@sabreskills.com
www.sabreskills.com

Sabre Business Skills is based in beautiful Richmond, British Columbia, Canada. The vision of the company is to empower people by giving them the skills they need to present themselves and their ideas in a very professional and powerful way. Why teach presentation skills AND business skills? Founder and program developer Kristina Schwende feels that you simply cannot have one without the other: "Teaching someone how to structure a great presentation is enhanced exponentially if they are able to present themselves in a manner that is truly professional. That way people can hear what they have to say without being distracted by what they are wearing or how they are conducting themselves."

Kristina Schwende has over 25 years experience in both the private and public sectors. She is a graduate of the esteemed Protocol School of Washington® where she received her certification as a Corporate Etiquette and International Protocol Consultant. She also received her training certification through Peak Potentials Training—a company recognized internationally for its professional and personal development programs.

High-Tech Etiquette

By Shery Scott

Appropriate etiquette, particularly business attire, varies from industry to industry. For example, the daily dress code for law firms and finance companies is very conservative: formal business. The technology industry, by contrast, has two different standards: business casual for the executives (customer-facing) and a much more casual standard for the engineering team (non-customer-facing), where jeans and sneakers tend to dominate on an average workday. While proper etiquette is crucial in all business interactions, it is important to note that different industries have different rules and standards. Because the technology industry is unique and widespread, we have chosen to give it special consideration and attention in our book so that you can succeed in this industry.

Before I dive into the differences in protocol, let's look at what makes the high-tech industry different in composition and culture. First, the people who make up the engineering team are more likely to be introverted than extroverted, even though in the population at large, extroverts outnumber introverts three to one, as discussed by Marti Olsen Laney in her book, *The Introvert Advantage*, published in 2002 by Workman Publishing. By contrast, the executives (management) are predominantly extroverts. So the composition of a technology company tends to have a small group of extroverted executives managing a large number of introverted engineers.

In *Executive Image Power*, published in 2009 by PowerDynamics Publishing, Kathryn Lowell, AICI CIP, confirmed what I have observed throughout my career. We need to "understand that our business culture rewards individuals who show extroverted qualities." Since executives like to get decisions made predominantly in meetings, and engineers tend to resist face-to-face communication—meetings in particular, preferring email instead—the differing communication styles of each group can create a challenging work environment for all.

Another characteristic of the technology industry is that it is extremely male-dominated, particularly the engineering team. When I was working for a software security firm in Silicon Valley, it was not at all unusual for me to be in a conference room with fifteen people and be the only woman. The downside of this lopsided gender representation is that women, who have historically been viewed as more nurturing and therefore more likely to excel in the soft skills, such as appropriate etiquette, are often expected to become somewhat masculine in their physical appearance, attire, and mannerisms in order to fit into the culture. In her February 2009 *Harvard Business Review* article, "Just Because I'm Nice...Don't Assume I'm Dumb," Amy J.C. Cuddy identified the reason for this expectation:

"People tend to see warmth and competence as inversely related. If there's an apparent surplus of one trait, they infer a deficit of the other. 'She's so sweet...she'd probably be inept in the board room.'"

Unfortunately, this also applies to technical skills, not just executive skills.

Business Attire for Men

As stated earlier, the engineering team may dress very casually on a daily basis, and it's my observation that this becomes increasingly true the farther west one travels. While engineers in the Midwest tend to adhere to business casual, West Coast dwellers prefer jeans, sneakers, and even T-shirts. Customer-facing employees, particularly the executive team, will remain in business casual attire, except on Fridays, graduating to business dress only when a customer is present.

This is also true for interviews. The rule of thumb is that the way a candidate appears during an interview is "as good as it gets." In other words, candidates applying for customer-facing positions should break out their interview suits, and make every effort to impress the interviewers. Candidates for non-customer-facing positions, on the other hand, can easily get away with a tailored shirt and slacks, with leather shoes. Grooming should be top-notch, in either case.

A friend told me the story of an unusually bright candidate who showed up for an interview in a T-shirt, shorts, and sneakers. Oddly enough he was hired, because he was so obviously competent for the job, but only with the strict understanding that he would never be in front of a customer. Even the door he used to enter and exit the building was completely outside a customer's view. Note, however, that his choice of attire cost him in the long run. He was ultimately unpromotable because of his choice in clothing. My recommendation? When in doubt, err on the side of conservatism. No one will ever discredit you for overdressing for an interview.

Business Attire for Women

As I mentioned earlier, it can be challenging to land an engineering position without sacrificing one's gender traits to some degree. Like the men in the industry, ladies need not adopt a blazer for a non-customer-facing position. Unlike them, we have a few more options. It used to be that an interview suit could only be a skirt suit. No longer. In the technology industry, women can interview in either a skirt or pants. Also, don't be afraid of color. The traditional black, grey, beige, or navy need not be your only options. Lighter blues, greens, and small plaids or prints can also be just as appropriate. In either case, keep the heels low—no more than two inches. Jewelry, too, should be kept to a bare minimum. Hair should be pulled back away from your face and preferably no longer than shoulder-length. And here's where you really need to be careful—keep the makeup to a bare minimum. In particular, avoid all bright colors. Neutral tones like soft grey and beige for eye shadow colors and muted, beige-toned lipsticks will serve you well.

Before I became familiar with such a relaxed attitude in the technology industry, I interviewed a candidate who came in wearing jeans and a loose sweater. While she may have been perfectly competent, I couldn't get over her casualness enough to give her any credibility.

Finally, the number of employees in a company can also determine how formally or informally a candidate can dress. The general rule of thumb is that the larger the company, the more formally you should dress. I recently went to a meeting at a company of 60 employees. I was wearing a skirt, a printed top, and a casual jacket, and I was the best-dressed person I saw in the building. When you go to meet with your clients and potential clients in technology companies, you can be the best-dressed person in the building, too. However, in most cases, you can still achieve that status while dressing down a little yet still wearing business casual.

Expressing Thanks

People with good soft skills are often unfairly judged as being less than competent in technical skills. In the technology field, when you express thanks, just as in other areas of good social etiquette, you'll want to strike the right balance. So be careful not to overdo it. For men in particular, handwritten thank-you notes may be viewed by the recipient as too personal, and could easily be misconstrued as a come-on, whether the recipient is male or female. Women, on the other hand—again, typically seen as more competent in the soft skills—can send handwritten thank-you notes when the occasion truly warrants it, and the recipient will likely interpret that thank-you note exactly as the sender intended. Ordinarily, though, your best bet is a brief email, or a face-to-face thank-you. If someone really goes over the top for you, offer to take him to lunch, or send him a gift card from Starbucks® or the iTunes® online store.

When It Is Appropriate to Get Personal

Departments within an organization can be very team-oriented and will often socialize together outside office hours. In fact, when I was a technical writer, the technical writing team and I went out to lunch together every day, and attended Shakespeare in the Park performances for several weekends. Of course, anyone who does not wish to share his or her personal time with the team should have his wishes respected.

When you have technology clients, do not think it strange if they invite you to the office for a meeting and you end up playing a game of ping-pong or pool before you leave. Because people in the technology industry are used to working such long hours, they often have fun while at work so they can go back to their desks feeling refreshed.

Remember that technology teams are made up mostly of introverts, and so your normal way of extending yourself and being personable may be rebuffed. It is seldom appropriate to get personal with anyone outside your own group, but there are exceptions. As a technical writer I was not in the "inner circle" of the engineering team, but I wanted to do something special for the engineer whose mother had recently passed away. So the whole technical writing team pitched in for a houseplant and a card, a small token of our sympathy, which I left on his desk. The thank-you email he sent me was one of the most heartfelt expressions of gratitude I have ever received. I was truly touched, and apparently, so was he. The bottom line here is that you can express your good intentions without invading someone's privacy.

Company-Sponsored Social Events

In the technology industry, particularly when the economy is strong, company-sponsored social events are common. Typically, these types of events are very informal, but the dress code and code of conduct still are in force. So keep your attire modest and watch the amount of drinking you do.

If you work at a company that is hosting a special event, attend it to show your company spirit and loyalty. There is an unspoken rule that attendance is mandatory, but you won't be expected to stay for the full event. Stay long enough to know that you have been seen by a majority of the employees. It's also a good idea to take the time to chat with the CEO and anyone else who cares about your attendance before leaving.

If your client invites you to their event, even if it seems like something that does not interest you, be sure to go. Flexibility and a willingness to have fun are very valued in the technology industry, since everyone works so hard.

Here is another example of the differences in personal interaction between introverts and extroverts. To over-generalize, the extroverts (management) love these types of social events and the introverts (engineering team) hate them. The purpose is to encourage social interaction and provide an environment conducive to teambuilding by adding some element of competition. One summer, our company sponsored a day in the park. Each team was to build a kite, which we later had to prove to be flight-worthy. While this may sound simple, it was actually rather challenging. With one or more "strong" personalities (extroverts) on the team, the social interaction can stall because the introverts will withdraw, and then the project may show less than stellar results. If you're an extrovert, you'll do well with introverts by addressing them individually rather than as a group. If you're an introvert, make an extra effort to be a little more light-hearted and social. By making a few adjustments in communication style, everyone will have the opportunity to participate and make a better contribution to the team.

Preferred Communication Methods

Unless you really need a meeting to get agreement among several people simultaneously, or the information you need to communicate is so detailed that it's easier to do face-to-face, use email whenever possible. While it may prove challenging to get a response from some of your recipients as quickly as you would like, you will score points by not interrupting the workday any more than is necessary. Introverts generally prefer to communicate to one person or to a very small group of people, and can feel anxious in a conference room crowded with people. In other words, introverts love email and prefer it to a phone conversation or a group conference call.

Also, in both emails and verbal communication, remember to be very explicit, specific and clear. Whoever said, "You're stating the obvious," and intended that as a put-down, did us all a great disservice. Because we tend to have very differing skill sets and functions within an organization, it would be dangerous to assume anything is obvious. What may be obvious to you won't be to someone else. Particularly in writing, don't be afraid to state what may seem to be common knowledge. You will probably find that the more completely you state the issues, the more useful your documents and emails, and ultimately you, will be.

While it's easy to get aggravated when faced with conflicting requirements, scarce resources, or other challenges, guard your professional reputation. Keep your communication, both verbal and nonverbal, devoid of emotion. No one wants to work with someone who is so unpredictable that he flies off the handle or is otherwise not emotionally self-controlled. Of course, if you do blow it, make your apologies as quickly as possible. Expressing remorse is a valuable relational skill and will go a long way toward improving all your working relationships.

Finally, never underestimate the power of a great sense of humor. On more than one occasion, I have become frustrated with people in meetings who were all talking at the same time. When that happens, it makes it nearly impossible for me to take notes. One time, I was on a conference call, trying to get two of the sales guys to back off and let the other speak. When I asked them to please stop talking on top of each other, one of them simply replied, "Oh no, we're arguing; we have to talk on top of each other." That completely diffused the tenseness of the situation, and I started laughing so hard, I had to put the phone down. If you can offer those unexpected, funny remarks that can erase a potentially problematic confrontation, your sense of humor will make those who tend to avoid confrontation see you as a valuable ally. The ability to put others at ease can be very valuable.

In conclusion, the more introverted and male-dominated work environments of the technology industry call for more informal business attire and somewhat less verbal communication. By taking these parameters into account with even a moderate mastery of the area of etiquette, you can succeed within technology environments.

SHERY SCOTT
Writer, Speaker, Trainer

(510) 508-4777
shery@hightechetiquette.com
www.hightechetiquette.com

Shery Scott was born into a strict military family and jokes that she could say ma'am and sir even before she could say mama and papa. However, she has a mother with a natural flair for Southern hospitality, and that became the foundation of Shery's etiquette training.

As a child of the military, Shery has traveled throughout the U.S. and abroad, learning the traditions, customs and social etiquette of other countries along the way. As an adult, she received her Bachelor of Science degree in computer science, with a minor in technical writing. She has been working as a technical writer in the technology industry for over 20 years, and as a technical trainer for the past 18 years.

Shery has also served as a volunteer trainer and group leader in the Celebrate Recovery ministry at Creekside Church in San Leandro, California, for the past five years. She received her certification to teach etiquette from the International School of Protocol in Hunt Valley, Maryland.

Primed with Professional Protocol

Hosting International Clients and Business Travel Abroad

By Listi A. Sobba

Your largest potential client has just scheduled a full tour of your company and three days of meetings with your entire organization. You know your product is high-quality, and you are well ahead of the competition. Still, you are worried. Your guests are from Pakistan, most of them do not speak English and they have never traveled in your region. How will you be certain they will feel completely capable of conducting business with you? What if they invite you to visit Pakistan? Does anyone on your team have experience traveling in this region? Priming yourself and your team with the rules of professional protocol will put you all at ease, reassure your guests and ultimately bring you the success you desire.

You may think the rules of protocol are only necessary if you are hosting royalty or foreign diplomats. On the contrary, protocol is imperative to the career of every corporate professional striving for success. More than ever, the global marketplace is accessible to businesses of every size and reach. You have the potential to capture clients from every corner of the world, and proficient protocol skills will help you enter this expanding global marketplace with confidence and competence.

The Purpose of Protocol

By definition, international protocol is a code of cultural behavior and procedures governed by international custom and practice that encourages respect and courtesy. Protocol, as a whole, is the observation of cultures and customs and includes greetings, gestures, dress and daily rituals. It is knowledge of forms of address and order of precedence. The giving of gifts is guided by the standards of protocol. There are protocols to follow when you and your client do not speak the same language, and protocol can help you to manage a translator properly. You can be certain to maintain appropriate topics of conversation by following protocol.

Observing international protocol will build a foundation of common understanding between you and your foreign clients. Protocol defines the circumstances you are about to enter. Without saying a word, you will be able to put your clients at ease and initiate clear communication. Protocol is your first step in establishing trust and respect in a business relationship. When I served as Assistant Manager of Blair House, the U.S. Presidents' Guest House, a great amount of attention was given to the rules of protocol before our guests took their first step through the front door.

Putting Protocol into Practice

Being professionally equipped with protocol does not mean you must be an expert in all world cultures, history or language. It does, however, require that you be knowledgeable about the customs, culture, current events and history of the country or region in which you wish to successfully conduct business. Your unawareness will cause you to appear uninterested, uninformed and/or arrogant. As Protocol Director for The Department of the Treasury, I prepared a document of protocol guidelines for each country on the Treasury Secretary's travel itinerary. This same type of briefing paper is prepared for the President of the United States every time he travels abroad and when a foreign visitor is scheduled to meet with him in the Oval Office.

It is not only important that the CEO or company's president be primed with this information, but that every level of your staff and team is ready to interact with your clients professionally and with genuine consideration for the differences. In the case of the President and Secretary of the Treasury, briefing papers were prepared in advance and distributed to the team of staff members who traveled in advance of the delegation to organize the logistical details necessary to prepare our Principals. This group of individuals gave the first impression and set the tone for the entire trip and the coming negotiations. Likewise, it is important to educate every member of your team—that means including the doorman and/or security officer—about basic greetings, taboo gestures and general culturally sensitive conduct.

Prepare a professional protocol briefing for yourself and your team each time you host international guests or travel abroad. Below are the components I consider to be most critical to the understanding of your potential business partner's culture and expectations. Each of the following criteria is presented using general guidelines. It is imperative that you understand that every culture is distinct, and so you must do additional research pertaining to your client's country specifically. Also, bear in mind that the results of that research are generalizations about the country's citizens. Your client is an individual and may not fit the mold precisely as you have defined it.

Have Basic Knowledge of Historical Highlights, Government Structure and Current Events

A country's history often evokes great pride in its citizens. Therefore, knowing its historical highlights will help you better understand your client, their needs and perhaps their agenda. The United States has a rich history that reflects a strong and stable country; we often take this for granted and are unaware of how our lives and culture would be different in an unstable environment. Your counterpart may be weighing issues such as border disputes, political unrest or relations with other countries when negotiating and making decisions with you. Additionally, I include several maps in my briefings, starting with the broadest image of the country and focusing in on the cities and venues to be visited. If you appear ignorant of a country's geography and its direct effect on the industry or company, that will translate to apathy toward the client and their business.

Educate yourself on the type of government that rules your client's country, how it was established and its stability. At Blair House, knowing that we would be hosting a king and a delegation ruled by a monarchy gave us great insight into the odd behavior and seemingly outlandish requests of our guests. Research the names of the country's national leaders and their titles; is it President, Prime Minister or King? It may be helpful to know the names of local government leaders and the national minister who oversees your area of interest.

As a businessperson, you know how the current state of the U.S. economy, political changes, holidays, notable sporting events, natural disasters and national or local events all affect your success or failure. It is the same situation in countries abroad, and therefore it is beneficial for you to be aware of current local events affecting your client. Consider spending time reading the Internet version of local newspapers that represent the region.

Be Aware How Various Gestures and Body Language are Interpreted

In which country does thumbs up mean money? In which country is thumbs up vulgar and rude? In which country does it mean, "You go first"? Similarly, you may be confused if do not know that your Albanian clients will shake their heads from side to side to indicate yes and nod their heads up and down to mean no. You may risk offending your clients from Arabic countries if you offer your left hand or reveal the sole of your shoe when crossing your legs. While some body language may seem universal and inconsequential, many gestures have conflicting meanings in one culture versus another. When interacting with international clients, educate yourself and your staff on the use of hand movements, acceptable physical contact, degrees of personal space and appropriateness of eye contact.

Additionally, I've listed a few general guidelines you should observe to avoid being offensive or misunderstood:

- Keep your voice at a moderate level and do not speak loudly.
- Maintain proper posture and do not put your hands in your pockets.
- Never display affection in public, pat anyone on the back or touch the head. Keep touching to a minimum in all situations.
- Do not point or make direct hand gestures.
- Be cautious and remember, even a smile can be interpreted in many different ways.

Respect Customary Dress and Choose Appropriate Attire

As you have seen, there are countless ways in which businessmen and businesswomen from different cultures may misunderstand each other during the course of meeting. However, how you choose to dress is completely in your control. Therefore, when meeting with international clients, it is wise to dress conservatively and in a traditional business suit unless you are invited to do otherwise. While you should never attempt to mimic the native dress of your clients, you should be aware of cultural sensitivities. For example, when we hosted guests from Arabic countries at Blair House, I kept in mind their culture requires that women be covered from head to toe with an abaya. Therefore, I chose loose-fitting suits whose hemline was below the knee and paired them with shirts that had high necklines. I could feel comfortable that I was modestly covered and not offending our guests, while still dressed in American style.

As a host to international visitors, the comfort level of your guests will have a direct correlation to the productivity of the meetings taking place. When you are arranging meetings, meals and entertainment, your visitors will appreciate being told specifically how to dress for the occasion. If the meetings are to be held at a resort in South Florida, "casual dress" is not enough information. Clarify if a sports coat is expected or if a golf shirt is sufficient. Likewise, as a guest, if you are uncertain of the attire, it is entirely appropriate to inquire of your host.

Understand Rank, Proper Use of Titles and Pronunciation of Names

Seniority and rank are highly regarded in most countries and should be well considered by your team. Moreover, it is important to note that this status may be based on a variety of criteria. A foreign guest at a social event or meeting will expect to be seated with people of comparable rank. During my time at The Department of the Treasury, we hosted high level Chinese government officials for the U.S. and China Strategic Economic Dialogue. Each of our Cabinet Secretaries participated in these series of meetings, as did their Chinese counterparts. Cabinet Secretaries were seated across the table from the corresponding Minister, and each side was carefully arranged according to the order or precedence set by each country. It was a puzzle to pair counterparts together when the corresponding ministries did not rank equally in the respective countries.

Additionally, one's title is a great indicator of status, and has significance that should be understood. Knowing there is great pride and sensitivity in one's title, you should address your client using official titles followed by his or her last name. Never refer to someone simply by his or her first name unless invited to do so. Also be aware that names are not always written in the same order as they are in the United States. When preparing your briefings, it is helpful to write out the names of your hosts or visitors phonetically, and the order in which they should be spoken. If you are ever in doubt, it is best to ask for clarification rather than misspeak, and always err on the side of formality.

Learn the Native Language and Know How to Use a Translator

It is not necessary to take a crash course in Arabic, nor is it realistic to try to learn a new language each time you pitch a new international client. However, consider learning a few basic words in your client's native language. This attempt will demonstrate your sincerity and show your clients that you are interested in their culture. When preparing to greet official visitors of the Treasury Secretary or guests at Blair House, I learned how to greet, say hello, please and thank you in the native language of our visitors. It is especially important to be able to thank your host when traveling abroad; learning these few words will surely show that you care.

When conducting international business, language translators are vital assets. They are most effective when you create a partnership with them and observe certain courtesies. If possible, meet with the translator before the appointment to ask his or her guidance on specific protocol and cultural expectations. Give the translator an outline for the discussion and share your goals for the meeting. Remember to speak slowly, use simple language and short sentences. Pause often and repeat the most pertinent information. Direct your remarks to your client. Always assume they can understand English; never say anything that you would not want them to hear.

Be Conscious of Conversational Guidelines and Topics to Avoid

As previously mentioned, acquainting yourself with current events, national history and local treasures will show your interest in the country. Moreover, it will improve your conversational skills. Sociable conversation is the best way to build good rapport and secure relationships. You are encouraged to ask questions of your counterpart; however, inquiries should be approached with sensitivity and consciousness. Understand that there are topics you are advised to avoid. It is best to refrain from discussions about money, country comparisons, health, religion and extremely personal questions. Jokes do not translate well and are best excluded from conversation. It is typically acceptable to discuss sports, art, music and history. The most favorable topics are those relating to your client's country; ask about holidays, local foods, or comment on the beauty of the country and its local attractions. The more research and knowledge you have gathered about the country, the broader, more interesting and confidently appropriate your topics of conversation will be. For example, when traveling to Kuwait, your protocol briefing will certainly warn your team not to bring up the subject of women or the topic of Israel, and when in Mexico, you will be encouraged to inquire about your client's family and share the joys of your own family.

Know the General Pace, Work Schedule and Expectations of Punctuality

The cultural concept of punctuality and the outlook on time and pace varies as much as the flavors of food and the language of tribes. In general, Americans operate on a faster pace than most cultures. You will find the sense of urgency less and the time it takes to make decisions and meet deadlines much longer. In some countries, it is truly impolite to arrive at the invited time, while in others it may be standard practice to keep you waiting so long that you should not expect to schedule more than one meeting a day. Yet elsewhere, tardiness is such a negative sign that it may eliminate you as a viable candidate for business. As a guest in a country, you should always arrive on time for a business meeting. You may be kept waiting, but do not be offended. On the other hand, social events adhere to a different code of conduct; inquire specifically about when you are expected to arrive.

When traveling or corresponding with your prospective client, it is important to consider the time of year, as seasonal weather patterns and traditional vacation time may make it impossible to fulfill your agenda. For example, it is difficult to conduct business in New Zealand during December and January because most people are on summer vacation; this is also true of Europeans in August. Similarly, the workweek or daily schedule may vary. In Muslim countries, the workweek is Saturday to Wednesday; few people work on Thursday or Friday. Peru operates on a six-day workweek with a long midday break; all businesses are closed between the hours of 1 p.m.-3 p.m.

When hosting international guests, you may conduct business on the traditional timetable, but it would be considerate to create a flexible schedule that takes into account religious practices or customary routines.

Follow Gifting Guidelines

Gift giving is a universal custom. In business affairs, it is a way of welcoming guests, showing gratitude for hospitality and demonstrating eagerness to build relationships. It is more significant in some cultures than others, but every gift can carry a weighty implication that should be carefully considered. The gift itself is key, but how it is presented, to whom it is given, the timing of the exchange and the circumstances under which it is given are also critical. Even the color of wrapping paper carries a message that could have consequences. Often you will encounter a situation in which you will need to distribute gifts to more than one person in a group. It is acceptable to give people of the same status the same gift, but you are advised to give gifts of higher value to those at higher levels and tier down appropriately.

Generally, it is best to give gifts of high quality that are not grandiose. Gifts should reflect the level of the business relationship. If possible, put effort into choosing a personalized gift. When preparing gifts for the Treasury Secretary to give to his counterparts, I did extensive research on the receiving individual's interests, tastes, and background so that the gifts showed sincerity. We gave gifts that were made in America and represented Washington, D.C., The U.S. Department of the Treasury or the Secretary's own personality and hobbies. Gifts should be personalized, but never personal or intimate. Distinguish between gifts given as hostess gifts during a social event and those given during a business appointment.

Your protocol briefing should include a detailed list of the meetings you have scheduled, the corresponding gifts and when they should be given. It is imperative to pack extra gifts for your trip and to keep a gift stowed away in your briefcase for unexpected situations. Keep a record of the gifts given to you and, most importantly, reply promptly with a handwritten thank-you note.

The Promise of Protocol

With your protocol briefing in hand and the confidence that your team has been fully educated on proper protocol procedures, you can be sure your company and product will be stepping smartly onto the international corporate stage. Your client will be at ease and your display of respect will open clear communication and begin building the foundation for a lasting and promising relationship. With your knowledge of protocol, you will have the tools to succeed in the global marketplace and your business potential will be endless.

For detailed information about doing business in China and India, see Syndi Seid's chapter, *Eight Good Luck Tips for Proper Chinese Etiquette,* on page 215, and Sangeeta Sindhi Bahl's chapter on *The Art of Doing Business in India* on page 227, respectively.

LISTI A. SOBBA
Sobba Public, LLC

(202) 285-4478
listisobba@sobbapublic.com
www.sobbapublic.com

Listi Sobba is a consultant to corporate professionals and government officials in the area of international business and professional protocol. She is a certified Protocol Officer and an expert in hosting international clients and guests. She combines her skills and experiences to blend protocol with practicality.

Listi served in President George W. Bush's Administration as Director of Protocol at The United States Department of the Treasury; Assistant Manager at Blair House, the President's Guest House; in White House Oval Office Operations; and as an Advisor to the Under Secretary of State for Public Diplomacy and Public Affairs. Throughout her career she has worked with notable figures such as: His Holiness, Pope Benedict XVI; Presidents George H.W. Bush and George W. Bush; Prime Minister Gordon Brown; President Hamad Karzai of Afghanistan; King Mohammed VI of the Kingdom of Morocco; and Vice Premier of the People's Republic of China, Madam Wu Yi. After her years of public service and unique experiences, Listi joined Sobba Public, Inc.

Listi is a graduate of the University of Texas and The Protocol School of Washington®. She is a member of Protocol and Diplomacy International—Protocol Officers Association (PDI).

214

Eight Good Luck Tips for Proper Chinese Etiquette

By Syndi Seid

"However long a man has known his friends, he should always treat them with the same scrupulous courtesy. In this way, familiarity will not breed contempt but greater admiration."
—Confucius

Many people grew up believing in the Golden Rule, which states: "Do unto others as you would have them do unto you." Unfortunately, this rule no longer holds true in all cases, given that we now live in a world of great diversity. No longer does everyone come from similar backgrounds, and we cannot rely on being well received when we treat others by the Golden Rule.

This is especially true in China. Consider a new saying and principle that has emerged called The Platinum Rule, as formulated by Dr. Tony Alessandra, which states,

"Treat others the way they want to be treated."

We must all practice this new global principle in order to make new friends and influence the people with whom we want to do business throughout the world.

We all have a tendency to become too casual when it comes to our business interactions. Yet we must keep The Platinum Rule in mind daily, especially when dealing with the Chinese and other unfamiliar cultures. To that end, here are eight important tips for maximizing your success and luck when doing business in China.

1. Make the Best First Impression

How you present yourself in the initial minutes of meeting someone makes all the difference in the world—all over the world. It is definitely a fact of life. We all form snap decisions about whether we will like or dislike someone. To dismiss this intuition as unimportant would be the biggest mistake you could make in doing business globally, particularly in China.

The question then becomes: Will you be smart enough to take the necessary time and effort to find out how to ensure you make a great first impression in China?

Do your homework. Read books about China and the Chinese, interview friends who have traveled to China, or hire an etiquette coach to advise you how to have the most effective business interactions with the Chinese.

Never attend a meeting or event unprepared. It is important to keep in mind what kind of event you are attending and the purpose the host intends to achieve.

2. Be Extremely Savvy about Business Cards

The Chinese believe that the exchange of business cards is an extension of introducing yourself. So whether you are traveling the world or simply conducting business in your own hometown, the Asian ritual of the business card exchange is now considered part of global business protocol.

Remember to bring enough business cards. Whether you are traveling in the United States or abroad, always carry a minimum of three times the number of cards you think you need for the number of days you will be traveling, along with notes about the types of meetings and events you will be attending.

Presenting Business Cards

Always present your card using your right hand or both hands. Face the person to whom you are giving the card. Your right thumb or both thumbs will be showing, with the card held between your thumb and curled index finger(s). It is not appropriate to pass out cards as though you are dealing cards at a poker game. Whenever you present your card with both hands, it is the highest form of respect that signifies you are presenting yourself, on paper, as on a silver platter.

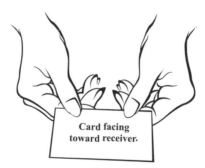

Card facing toward receiver.

Never present a card with your left hand, even if you are left-handed. Doing so is considered a total insult, indicating you truly don't care about doing business with the person or value them as a friend. This is especially true in the Muslim culture.

Remember that cards should always be in clean, pristine condition.

Receiving Business Cards

Always receive a card in the same manner as you presented yours—either in the right hand or with both hands, but never with the left hand.

Never take a business card and immediately put it aside. Take time to study the card. This is your golden opportunity to help yourself remember the person long after your meeting. Ask a question or make a nice comment about the card. After a few moments of conversation, put the card away appropriately, either in your purse, your briefcase, or best, in your upper breast pocket or jacket pocket.

Remember, never place cards in your trouser pockets, your back pocket or your wallet. When you do that and then sit down, it is just as though you are sitting on the person's face!

Pronouncing Names Correctly

Always take time while studying a business card to learn how to pronounce a person's name correctly. When you see an unusual or difficult name, ask, "Tell me, am I pronouncing your name correctly? Is it "Sid-ney Si-ed?" This allows the person to reply, "No, my name is actually pronounced like this: Cindy Seed."

Never ask, "Say, what's your name again?" or, "Wow, what kind of name is this?"

Remember that even if you are unable to repeat the name correctly after a second try, you are showing interest in the person by attempting to pronounce her name correctly.

Writing on Business Cards

It is natural to want to make notes on a business card, especially when the person asks you to send them a brochure. Be careful, though—never write on the face of the card, especially when you're standing in front of the person. It is as though you are writing on the person's face. Instead, make notes on a note pad or wait until you are out of sight of the person.

Keeping Business Cards

Always keep the business cards you receive in a separate card case. Don't ever use rubber bands or paper clips, which always dent the cards. If you have a special carrying case, it demonstrates that you respect the people who have just given you their cards.

Never ask a person for another card because you lost the first one. It is perceived that you have lost their face. Put the cards into your carrying case right away for safekeeping.

Remember to never keep cards in your trouser pockets, back pocket, or wallet.

3. Entertaining in China

Throughout time, the breaking of bread together has been an important ritual to establish mutual respect and trust. It is important to understand the significance of such practices, regardless of where you travel in the world, especially in China. If you don't adhere to certain practices at the dining table, you will not be invited to the negotiating table.

Always allow the host to take the lead in entertaining you, the chief guest, otherwise known as the guest of honor. When you attend an event, or any meeting, always be punctual. As a host or chief guest, you don't want to arrive after the other guests.

Never flatly refuse an invitation. Refusing an invitation is considered an insult. When absolutely necessary, suggest an alternate date and time when another appointment cannot be changed. Then apologize profusely for this inconvenience.

Always as the chief guest, reciprocate in kind by inviting your Chinese counterparts to a banquet or meal of equal value and quality. The new trend is to invite your Chinese hosts to experience a form of Western dining that will be new to them. For example, if you are German, take them to a German restaurant, or if you are American, take them to an American-style steakhouse. This will be the ultimate demonstration of how much you care about the relationship, and will be an experience they will remember for a lifetime.

Remember that business is rarely discussed at banquets unless the host brings it up first. Even then, the discussion is usually kept on the lighter, more general side. You can then talk about the arts, the delicious food, or the wellbeing of family members during the meal. As in all cultures, it is best not to discuss politics or religion at mealtime.

Be aware that no matter how long you have known someone in China, you may never be invited to their home. All entertaining is done at restaurants and other venues.

4. Don't Be Afraid of Chopsticks

Always give chopsticks a chance. Have fun practicing the manipulation of what is most likely the world's oldest eating utensil.

Never refuse to use chopsticks, as it is considered rude and shows how inflexible you are, not even to try.

Remember to learn how to use chopsticks before any trip to China or certainly before having a business meal with the Chinese. However, don't be shy to start using chopsticks when you get to China. The fact that you are willing to practice at every meal shows you are a person who is eager to learn new things and determined to succeed. This will win you praise and admiration—not to mention that you will be the source of great entertainment for the other diners during the evening.

5. How to Use Chopsticks

Always keep your chopsticks even to be able to use them properly. But do not hit your chopsticks on your plate or the table to get them even. Either even them up with your hands or discreetly place them in your mouth to even them up with your tongue.

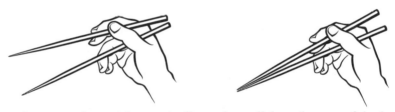

Never lay your chopsticks vertically and parallel on the top of the bowl or leave them sticking straight up in the bowl. This placement is considered a sign of bad luck, as it is used in ceremonies honoring the dead. Try never to drop your chopsticks, as this is also a sign of bad luck.

Remember to use serving chopsticks or spoons whenever available. If they are not available, use the top (wider) end of your chopsticks, not the end that goes into your mouth, to lift food from serving dishes onto your plate.

6. Be Courteous When Dining

Always wait for the host to begin before you start eating or drinking. In Chinese etiquette, the host always begins each dish by serving the chief guest and one or two other guests nearby.

Always taste a bite of every dish. Your host will be looking at you to see your fortitude. Unless you are allergic to a food, or it is against your religious or dietary restrictions, you may not refuse to taste, and don't lie either. To say you can't stand the thought of eating that fish eyeball would be considered a total insult and most selfish. As long as you know it is not poison, try it; you might like it.

Pace yourself and eat lightly throughout the meal. Don't feel you have to eat everything on your plate, including your second or third helpings. If you leave a clean plate, the host will think you are still hungry and will feel obliged to serve you still more helpings of food. Conversely, leaving food totally untouched is offensive, as though it was not appealing.

Never pick up serving dishes or pass them around. Leave serving dishes on the table or lazy Susan. You can reach across the table to get food from a serving dish by bringing your plate close to the serving dish.

Never go through a dish, looking to grab a piece of food that appeals to you. Decide on the piece you want, and then use the serving chopsticks or the bigger ends of your chopsticks to get it.

Always offer someone else tea and food before you serve yourself. You would be considered to have bad manners if you serve yourself first.

When you notice food or drink being served to you by the dining partner next to you, signal your appreciation by gently tapping your index and middle finger put together, gently twice on the table. This gesture acknowledges what you have received yet won't interrupt other activities.

Never take the last piece of food on the serving platter. It's considered bad luck, shows greed and you seem too hungry. Offer the piece to others.

Never put your hands in your mouth for any reason while at the table; it's considered disgusting. If you must take something out of your mouth, such as bones or gristle, use your chopsticks to remove the item and place it on the side of your plate. If you must use a toothpick, cover your mouth with your other hand before sticking the toothpick in your mouth.

Place bones and other discarded items on a side dish, that is usually on the table, never back in your rice bowl.

Remember that guests generally do not linger much past the end of the meal. The host typically encourages guests to take any uneaten food home. If you are offered food, take it. If you are the guest of honor, you should arrive first and leave first.

7. Making a Successful Toast
Always end a toast by saying "Gambei," which means dry glasses or bottoms up.

Never clink glasses. The Chinese custom is to show the utmost respect by lifting your glass and holding it with both hands to shoulder height when giving or receiving toasts.

Remember that to complete the toast, everyone is expected to drink everything in his or her glass, and often to turn the glass upside down to prove they drank it all. So, be sure to pace yourself and brace yourself—eat before the actual banquet and remain calm to get through the evening.

Whether at a small dinner event or a large banquet, the evening will always begin with brief comments or a speech by the host thanking guests for attending, and end with a welcome toast. As the chief guest, you will not return the toast immediately. Instead, you will wait until the second or third course to say a few words and toast the host and all of the other guests.

8. Know the Art of Giving Gifts

Always present gifts using both hands and receive gifts in both hands. Do not open gifts in front of others, unless you are encouraged to do so. Gifts are given as an expression of your feelings for a person or a group, not just for the sake of giving someone a gift.

Choose gifts with care. Do not give elaborate or extravagant gifts, as the Chinese may perceive this as a bribe. Instead, give practical and useful gifts, such as distinctive items for the office, specialty items or coffee table books. Other good gifts include French cognac and Scotch whiskey, and in recent years, American bourbons and wines. American-made chocolates are also a popular gift. Just make sure you aren't transporting chocolate in summer and that your gifts were not printed or made in any part of Asia.

Never wrap gifts in white paper as white is associated with death. Rather, wrap gifts in red or gold—not yellow—paper to be best received. Keep the wrapping simple, without lots of fancy bows or patterned paper. When traveling, do not wrap the gifts ahead of time. Instead pack the paper, ribbon and adhesive tape to wrap the gifts upon your arrival. This way, if your luggage is searched, the wrapping won't be ruined and the package will look its freshest.

Remember never give a clock or a knife. The word clock sounds like the word associated with pre-funeral visits for someone who has died, and knives are not a good gift because they are associated with killing.

Flowers are not a good gift either, because they are primarily given at funerals. Avoid food items, as the Chinese perceive this to mean you think they are hungry.

Here's a Question for You

Do you know why this chapter contained eight tips? Why not seven, nine, or ten tips? The answer is that eight is a good luck number in the Chinese culture.

Keep an open mind and be willing to try new things, especially regarding a country like China, which is so very different from western culture. If you plan to do business with the Chinese, make sure you incorporate these eight tips into your business practices, and know that you will be well on your way to becoming a global businessperson.

For more information on international etiquette, see Listi Sobba's chapter, *Primed with Professional Protocol,* on page 203.

SYNDI SEID
Advanced Etiquette[SM]

(415) 346-3665 or (800) 276-7419
info@advancedetiquette.com
www.advancedetiquette.com

Syndi Seid is an etiquette expert, corporate trainer, international author and speaker to the world's leading organizations and the media, providing comprehensive training and consulting on global business protocol and social etiquette.

As founder of Advanced Etiquette, Syndi helps senior executives and business professionals worldwide overcome their lack of awareness and skills to gain poise, confidence and authority in any situation, anywhere in the world.

Major companies such as Hewlett-Packard Worldwide, Sprint International, Marriott Hotels, and the Miss Universe Pageant trust Syndi to train their employees to avoid social *faux pas* that could lead to major business and political blunders.

Syndi has appeared on national and international television, including ABC's *Good Morning America*, CBS' *Eye on America*, and Fox's *Trading Spouses*, as well as on radio and in print. She is the Etiquette Expert for Staples.com, a contributing writer for Bnet.com, the technical editor for the second edition of the book *Business Etiquette for Dummies* and etiquette columnist for *AsianWeek*. She is the author of *Etiquette in Minutes: 201 Practical Tips for Business and Social Behavior,* and a co-author of *The Law of Business Attraction,* with T. Harv Eker.

The Art of Doing Business in India

By Sangeeta Sindhi Bahl, Executive MBA (UK), AICI FLC

"Everyone arriving in India for the first time wants to change the country; but when they leave they realize that it has changed them!"

—Anonymous

India is well on its way to fulfilling the projections made by Goldman Sachs, the world's top investment bank, that it will emerge as the third largest economy in two decades and the world's second largest economy by 2050, behind China, and ahead of the U.S.

India's rich cultural heritage, society and customs are key elements of doing business in India. By understanding and showing respect for how things are done in India, you will ensure that your business dealings will have a good chance of succeeding.

The Role of Family

We Indians largely define ourselves by the groups to which we belong rather than by our status as individuals. This group orientation arises from the close personal ties Indians maintain with their family, including the extended cousins and far-off relatives. The extended family creates a myriad of interrelationships, rules and structures.

It is vital for foreigners visiting India to remember that in general, important decisions are made not as individuals but as a family. The Indian family plays a pivotal role in shaping an individual's future at work and in important decisions like getting married. Unlike Western countries, even a decision such as taking a job abroad has to meet with the family's approval. At the core of Indian culture lies an innate respect for parents and other elders in the family; usually no major decision is taken without consulting them.

Understanding India's Hierarchical Society

Since India is a hierarchical culture, always greet the eldest or most senior person in a group first. When you are leaving, you must bid each person farewell individually.

Indian society is multifaceted to an extent probably unlike any other of the world's great civilizations. The influence of the largest tradition of the caste system of Hinduism has created a culture that emphasizes established hierarchical relationships. The patriarch, usually the father, is considered the leader of the family.

Every relationship has a clear-cut hierarchy that must be observed if the social order is to be maintained. Throughout India, individuals are also ranked according to their wealth and power.

Social interaction is regarded as being of the highest priority, and social bonds are expected to be long lasting. Even economic activities that might, in Western culture involve impersonal interactions are, in India, deeply imbedded in a social nexus. All social interaction involves constant attention to hierarchy, respect, honor, the feelings of others, rights and obligations, hospitality, and gifts of food, clothing and other desirable items. Finely tuned rules of etiquette help facilitate each individual's many social relationships.

Foreigners to India are sometimes startled to find that important government and business officials have left their posts—often for days at a time—to attend a far-off relative's joyous occasion or to participate in religious activities in a distant part of the country. "He is out of station and will be back in a week or two," the absent official's officemates blandly explain to the frustrated visitor. This is not laziness or hedonistic recreation. It is rather the official's proper recognition of his need to continually maintain his social ties with relatives, caste fellows, associates and God.

Religion

About 80 percent of India's population are Hindus. Hinduism is a colorful and ancient religion with a vast gallery of gods and goddesses. In India, religion is a way of life, an integral part of the entire Indian tradition. For the majority of Indians, religion permeates every aspect of life, from commonplace daily chores to education and politics. Secular India is home to Hinduism, Islam, Christianity, Buddhism, Jainism, Sikhism and other innumerable religious traditions.

In the shadow of Hindu dominance, and a Muslim community larger than the entire population of Pakistan, there are a few followers of other beliefs such as Christianity, Sikhism and Buddhism. The diversity of India makes it the most unique country in the world. The customs and rituals are an integral part of the culture, traversing the boundaries of religion, caste and creed.

Business Negotiations

Close familiarity with Indian business ethics can help you do business in India successfully. It is advisable to pay attention to the following:

- Indians are non-confrontational. It is rare for them to overtly disagree, although this is beginning to change in the managerial ranks.

- Decisions are made by the person with the most authority.

- Delays are to be expected, especially when dealing with the government.

- Most Indians expect concessions in both price and terms. It is acceptable to expect concessions in return for those you grant.

- Do not disagree publicly with members of your negotiating team.

- Never appear overly legalistic during negotiations. In general, Indians do not trust the legal system, and therefore someone's word is sufficient to reach an agreement. However, verbal acceptance must be followed by a written proclamation of the agreement that should be mutually accepted by both parties.

- Successful negotiations are often celebrated with a meal.

- Decision making in India is a slow process.

Communicating Cross-Culturally

Doing business in India successfully requires a variety of new skills and sets of knowledge. India's working culture and day-to-day management style are very different from the Western style, which leads to further confusion.

Indian mannerisms are very different from those in the West. One motion that is hard to decipher is the movement of the head to denote yes or no. Some Indians shake their head from side to side when they mean yes, while others move their head up and down to say yes and sideways to say no. Then there is a third head movement that is between a nod and a shake, and involves moving the head in a kind of a semicircular motion. It means yes too. Another sometimes perplexing practice is plain silence, which could be used to mean either *yes* or *no*.

Meeting and Greeting

In India, religion, education and social class influence all greetings. This is a hierarchical culture, so greet the eldest or most senior person first. In India, always introduce the senior person to the junior person as a mark of respect. When leaving a group, bid farewell to each person individually.

Shaking hands is common, especially in the large cities among the more educated who are accustomed to dealing with Westerners.

Men may shake hands with other men and women may shake hands with other women; however, there are seldom handshakes between men and women because of religious beliefs. If you are uncertain about what to do, wait for a person to extend their hand. With Indian women, wait for their initiative.

The traditional form of greeting in India, *Namaskar*, is based on a profound philosophy of non-arrogance or negation of ego. *Namaskar* is made of three words: *Namah + Om + kar = Namaskar*. *Namah* literally translated means "not me." It is a negation of one's identity, and hence of one's ego or arrogance. *Om* is the sound of life. It is believed that to begin with, there was only the sound of *om* and the whole world evolved from it. *Om* is often used in meditation. The whole cosmos is summed up in the word *om*.

Namaste is also used as a greeting. *Namaste* is made of two words: *namah + te = namaste*. In Sanskrit, *te* means "they." The literal meaning of *namaste* therefore is "Not me, they." It is the word that refers to all the gods. *Namaste* is hence a philosophical statement affirming that the doer of everything is not me, but the gods.

The Unspoken Rules of Business Meetings

In a meeting or group discussion, only the most senior person may speak. Others will often remain silent out of respect for him or for you. This does not necessarily indicate agreement with your views. But westernized Indians can be assertive and frank, and it is okay to use the same attitude with them. Politeness and honesty are important to demonstrate that your intentions are sincere and genuine.

Status is determined by age, university degree, caste and profession. If someone does not have a professional title, use the honorific title "Sir" or "Madam." Wait to be invited before using someone's first name alone, without the title.

Decisions are strongly influenced from the top. Usually one person makes all major decisions, so attempt to deal with the highest-level person available.

It is considered rude to plunge into business discussions immediately. Ask about your counterpart's family, interests, or hobbies before beginning business discussions.

Business is slow and difficult in India. Be polite, but persistent. Do not get angry if you are told something "can't be done." Instead, restate your request firmly, but with a smile. Plan on several visits before you reach an agreement. Since your Indian counterparts may not show up for scheduled meetings or may be delayed, be prepared to reschedule.

Appointments. In India, it is mandatory to make appointments before any business dealings take place.

Business Attire. Senior management in India wear suits. However, because of the climatic conditions, they sometimes dress less formally.

Business attire is conservative. Indian women wear ethnic attire for work. In most expatriate companies now, women are wearing both traditional attire and business suits.

Business Cards. Business cards are exchanged after the initial handshake and greeting.

• If you have a university degree or any other honor, print it on your business card.

• Always present your business card when introduced. Use your right hand to give and receive business cards.

Indians are Inquisitive and Extremely Hospitable

Even strangers want to know everything—what you do, what your parents do, what your children do, what you ate for dinner, even how much your house cost. This is one aspect of the Indian culture that is sometimes tough to understand. The key here is to look beyond the questions at the true intention. Knowing all about you is, for Indians, both a way of sizing you up as well as establishing a relationship with you.

You are extremely lucky if you get invited to an Indian home. The aroma of sizzling vegetables, warm curry, lentils, and rice greets guests as they enter the foyer of a traditional Indian home. Because the home is a reflection of an Indian family's life and pride, most Indians go to great lengths to make a visitor feel comfortable and secure. After all, Indian hospitality is a reflection of the family, their home, their culture and their country.

Although the chief male of the clan, usually the grandfather or great-grandfather, is the most prominent symbol of the family, the women are the backbone of traditional hospitality. Despite fulfilling her duty as a wife and a mother, a true Indian woman takes pride in herself, her family, and her house and will not let a guest go away unfed or unhappy.

An Indian woman shows her talents and her warmth through the food she serves, and is known for offering delicious fare to her guests, whether they are invited or not. As soon as a guest arrives, every amenity is offered. Traditionally, the best bed in the house is given to the honored guest.

Restaurant Dining Etiquette—Indian Food

In Indian life, among friends and in community gatherings, food is an indispensable part of socializing and an important aspect of any festivity. Sharing food establishes the concept of graceful give-and-take, and all other social interactions can be modeled upon this sharing.

Important cultural tip. The right hand is valued more in India than the left. It is considered inauspicious to accept anything with the left hand, especially cash and important documents. Most Indians eat food with the fingers of their right hand. Using a spoon is relatively common if you are eating off a plate, but if you are eating off a plantain leaf, as in some traditional households or at weddings, make sure you use only your right hand.

Restaurant dining is different from eating in a home. For starters, you are offered spoons and forks, even if many diners do not use them. In midrange-to-upscale restaurants, dining etiquette is similar to that in Western countries, but the tipping customs are somewhat different. Although everyone from the bellhop to the waiter expects and likes to be tipped, Indians are not very good tippers. Most Indians will tip much less than 10 percent of the total cost of the bill and sometimes none at all.

Things to Remember about Business Dining in India

Initial business entertainment is done in restaurants at prestigious hotels. Business can be discussed during meals, but allow your host to initiate the business conversation.

- Never flatly refuse an invitation to a home, or a business dinner from a business counterpart. If you can't make it, offer a plausible excuse.

- Spouses are often included in social business functions.

- Strict orthodox Muslims don't drink any alcohol. Most Hindus, especially women, do not consume alcohol.

- Arrive 15-30 minutes later than the stated time for a dinner party.

- Allow hosts to serve you. Never refuse food, but don't feel obligated to empty your plate. Hindu hosts are never supposed to let their guests' plates be empty.

- If your hosts eat with their hands, assure them you enjoy doing the same. If utensils are not used, only use the first three fingers (including thumb) of your right hand.

- Take food from a communal dish with a spoon; never use your fingers. Use chappati or puri (bread) torn into small chunks to scoop up food.

- The host pays for guests in a restaurant.

- Guests give gifts to the host and the host's children as a "thank you."

- You should reciprocate invitations with a meal of comparable value. Never invite someone to a far more lavish dinner—it might embarrass them.

It may surprise Westerners to see Indians eating their traditional food and even rice with their hands. This does not mean that they do not know how to use a fork and knife or are uncivilized. This is the way food is eaten and savored the most. If you also eat with your hands it will be very much appreciated and acceptable and a pleasant surprise for the Indian.

Gift Giving and Receiving

Indians place a great deal of importance on the family and respect those who value their family. Here are a few tips to help you navigate through this complex area:

- While visiting a home, taking a gift of sweets, fruits or a bouquet of flowers is considered a nice gesture.
- When presenting gifts, take care that the gift-wrapping is neither black nor white, as these are believed to bring bad luck.
- The colors that are thought to bring good luck are red, green and yellow.
- It is not customary in India to open a gift in the presence of its donor.
- Gifts of cash are given to friends and members of the extended family to celebrate life events such as birth, death and marriage.
- Do not give frangipani or white flowers, as they are used at funerals.
- A gift from a man should be said to come from both him and his wife/mother/sister or some other female relative.
- Hindus should not be given gifts made of leather.
- Indians believe that giving gifts eases the transition into the next life.

There are many advantages to living or doing business in India—the long-lasting friendships forged with Indians, the values that can be absorbed from Indian culture, the many breathtaking and unique places to visit, the wide assortment of cuisines available to regale your taste buds, and of course, the innumerable exotic knickknacks that can be bought. Anyone who is ready to recognize the cultural differences and make the necessary adjustments will certainly experience success in all his or her Indian business endeavors.

SANGEETA SINDHI BAHL,
Executive MBA (UK), AICI FLC
Impact Image Consultants

Unleash your potential and make
a stellar IMPACT!

0091-9810467788

sangeeta.sbahl@
impactimageconsultants.net

www.impactimageconsultants.net

Sangeeta Sindhi Bahl, Founder and Director of Impact Image Consultants, is a former airline professional, model, actress and now an image, etiquette and color consultant for both men and women. She is based in Gurgaon, India. In 2006, using her MBA business acumen and 24 years of international airline industry experience, she graduated from Image Maker Inc., founded by Dr. Joyce Knudsen, AICI CIM, completed her color training at Universal Color System in Australia, and trained in bridal, airbrush, fashion and ramp makeup at Kryolan Mephisto Makeup Academy in Germany.

Sangeeta is the first AICI Certified Image Consultant in India. Having worked extensively with Emirates, Thai International and Royal Jordanian airlines, and accustomed to dealing with royalty and international celebrities, etiquette and protocol are second nature to Sangeeta.

She customizes and creatively designs seminars and in-house presentations for both companies and individual clients. Her vivacious personality and practical, dynamic approach have helped clients discover and develop their own sense of identity and style with color, personality and lifestyle. Sangeeta instills in each client a sense that they are glamorous and very special.

More Executive Etiquette Power

Now that you have learned many things about how to conduct yourself in a wide variety of professional scenarios, the next step is to take action. Get started applying what you have learned in the pages of this book.

We want you to know that we are here to help you meet your professional and personal objectives.

Below is a list of where we are geographically located. Regardless of where our companies are located, many of us provide a variety of services over the phone or through webinars, and we welcome the opportunity to travel to your location.

You can find out more about each of us by reading our bios at the end of our chapters, or by visiting our websites listed on the next two pages.

When you are ready for one-on-one consulting or group training from any of the co-authors in this book—we are available! If you call us and let us know you have read our book, we will provide you with a free phone consultation to determine your needs and how to best serve you.

United States

Alabama
Dallas Teague Snider, CMP   www.businessetiquetteacademy.com

California
Linda Cain   www.mce-international.com
Barbara Khozam   www.barbarakhozam.com
Kim Maxwell   www.theetiquettelady.net
Shery Scott   www.hightechetiquette.com
Syndi Seid   www.advancedetiquette.com
Katherine Bessell Wurzburg, AICI FLC   www.thefinessefactor.com

District of Columbia
Vonetta Dumas   www.diverse-images.net
Holiday Johnson   www.holidayjohnson.com
Michele Pollard Patrick   www.nationalprotocol.com
Listi A. Sobba   www.sobbapublic.com

Illinois
Barbara Finney   www.etiquette-leadership.net

Louisiana
Suzanne Zazulak Pedro   www.theprotocolpraxis.com

New Jersey
Debra Gitto   www.etiquetteinfo.com

New York
Pamela Minyard, MS   www.pamelaminyard.com

Ohio
Kay Stephan   www.classicprotocol.com

Texas & Washington
Deborah King, AICI CIP   www.finaltouchschool.com

Canada

Alberta
Terry Pithers

www.styleforsuccess.com

British Columbia
Kristina Schwende, CEP

www.sabreskills.com

India

Haryana
Sangeeta Sindhi Bahl,
Executive MBA (UK), AICI FLC

www.impactimageconsultants.net

PowerDynamics Publishing develops books for experts who speak and want to share their knowledge with more and more people.

We know getting a book written and published is a huge project. We provide the resources, know-how and an experienced team to put a quality, informative book in the hands of our co-authors quickly and affordably. We provide books, in which our co-authors are proud to be included, that serve to enhance their business missions.

You can find out more about our projects at
www.powerdynamicspub.com